# FACING A WORLD IN CRISIS

*What Life Teaches Us in Challenging Times*

## J. KRISHNAMURTI

EDITED BY DAVID SKITT

SHAMBHALA
*Boston & London*
2005

Shambhala Publications, Inc.
Horticultural Hall
300 Massachusetts Avenue
Boston, Massachusetts 02115
www.shambhala.com

©2005 by Krishnamurti Foundation Trust, Ltd
Edited by David Skitt

For information about Foundations, Schools, and Study Centers, please contact:
Krishnamurti Foundation Trust
Brockwood Park
Bramdean, Hampshire
SO24 OLQ
info@brockwood.org.uk, www.kfoundation.org
or
Krishnamurti Foundation of America
P.O. Box 1560
Ojai, CA 93024-1560
kfa@kfa.org, www.kfa.org

9  8  7  6  5  4  3

Printed in the United States of America

⊗ This edition is printed on acid-free paper that meets the American National
Standards Institute Z39.48 Standard.
♻ This book was printed on 30% postconsumer recycled paper. For more
information please visit us at www.shambhala.com.
Distributed in the United States by Random House, Inc., and in Canada by
Random House of Canada Ltd

Library of Congress Cataloging-in-Publication Data
Krishnamurti, J. (Jiddu), 1895–
Facing a world in crisis: what life teaches us in challenging times / Jiddu
Krishnamurti—1st ed.
p.  cm.
ISBN 978-1-59030-203-3 (pbk.: alk. paper)
1. Life.  2. Conduct of life.  I. Title.
B5134.K753F33 2005
204'.4—DC22
2004016052

# Contents

# INTRODUCTION

Nowadays we know more about what is happening in the world than ever before. Global TV coverage means that every natural disaster, every war, every terrorist attack, every major sporting event is brought, often "live," before our eyes.

Although such reporting is often biased toward sensational events involving strife and death, it also forces us to face inescapably hard facts about the world we live in. Wars due to the savage mix of territorial disputes with religion and nationalism; the clash of cultures, each sure its values are universal; the new height of violence shown by suicide attacks are a daunting overture to a new millennium. They seem even more daunting when growing economic interdependence, environmental damage, conflict over water supplies, and climate change demand a new sense of shared interest, a new and vital human togetherness, if some kind of cataclysm is to be averted. The old loyalties to one's own country, religion, or political ideology seem dangerously at odds with a reality that demands loyalty to the human species as a whole, rather than to one's preferred segment of it.

Throughout the 1970s J. Krishnamurti, who had been talking

to audiences around the world for more than fifty years, began to speak repeatedly about looking at the state of the world as a first step in looking at the way each of us lives his or her life. To turn away from world events, to think that "what is going on *out there* has nothing to do with me," was for him not to be alive to what life has to teach, a fake retreat from the vast arena of human behavior where all of us are actors, whether we like it or not. To recoil from the world's violence and set ourselves apart—something we do not do, of course, with life's pleasures—was a serious misperception, a failure to see and to feel in our blood that "we are all in the same boat." This error, he maintained, would inevitably lead to ineffectual action and conflict.

This view, often expressed by Krishnamurti in the phrase "I am the world," has been stated by others. The philosopher Thomas Hobbes wrote, "Whosoever looks into himself shall know the thoughts and passions of all other men," and Montaigne said, "Every man carries in him the whole of the human condition." Not content with merely stating the maxim, Krishnamurti goes on to explore its implications in great depth and detail and to ask, since each of us is a participant, what our response is to the present insecure, disturbing state of the world.

But then he raises a more fundamental issue: What kind of a mind is *capable* of responding adequately to it? What are the obstacles to having such a mind? This is not unlike a scientist who before studying a phenomenon looks to the quality of the apparatus that will be used to observe it. In Part One of this book, Krishnamurti explores these obstacles. He suggests that insight into their nature not only brings about the right response to events in the world politically, economically, and religiously, but also reveals their psychological origins in our personal lives and relationships. Psychologically, the dividing line between the person and society disappears. Poetically, he often describes this as "the tide going out and the tide coming in."

What he says may disappoint readers who want pat answers from an authority whom they can then believe in. For Krishnamurti, to want this not only atrophies the brain but contributes dangerously to political and religious tyranny in the world. And in our personal relationships it may easily lead to one person dominating the other. What he gives us are not theories or explanations but statements to test against our experience or questions to kickstart our own inquiry. Life is something we need to explore for ourselves; it is greater, he says, than any teacher or teaching. To see it in any other way is to be a "secondhand human being."

Many people have called Krishnamurti a mystic, a word that can be used to grant him exalted status and/or to dismiss him as irrelevant. But what he says is time and again very relevant to personal relationships and to politics. In almost every talk he refers to the destructiveness of image making in the relationship between man and woman, and with regard to authoritarian political systems, it is of interest to note that historians have described their prerequisites as follows: First, there is the inculcation of a sense of "us" and "them"; second, willingness to conform; third, not opposing harm being done to "them" and passing responsibility for this on to the authorities, while assuming that "they" are not human in the way "we" are; fourth, not opposing the suppression of dissent; and fifth, not opposing, or going along with, extermination of "them." This is not just a psychological scenario for succumbing to political tyranny or for the persecution of an ethnic minority. It is also a psychological scenario that motivates a whole nation to go to war with another.

What does Krishnamurti say that challenges this sorry process? He points repeatedly to the unreality of the "them and us" distinction between human beings, the falseness of such images, and the neurotic allegiances they give rise to. While accepting that conformity to some rules is socially necessary, he sees conformity to and belief in political and religious authority—

including, as already pointed out, any attributed to him personally—as a form of social and psychological oppression stunting the brain. In doing so he is thus proposing potential barriers in us to the kind of political systems that wrought havoc in the twentieth century and whose seeds continue to be sown in the present one.

So though a mystic is usually defined as someone concerned with ultimate reality and truths beyond the intellect, and Krishnamurti was also very much concerned with these, the relevance of what he says to authoritarianism shows that at the same time he had his feet firmly on the ground. Indeed, one could say much more firmly on the ground than many of us who, considering ourselves wholly rational and not mystical at all, have succumbed to blind faith in leaders or beliefs that have led to human suffering on an unprecedented scale.

THOSE READING Krishnamurti for the first time may find his free-ranging discourses disconcerting. Though they are carefully sequenced, he always responds to questions from his audience, even in mid-flow and however irrelevant they may seem to the main theme of his talk. But often, as already mentioned, it is he, the speaker, who puts questions to the audience rather than, as is usually the case, the other way around. As will be seen, at times he firmly declines to answer his own questions. On other occasions, he maintains that the answer to the question is in the question itself and proceeds to explore its terms. And he constantly warns against agreeing or disagreeing intellectually with what he says rather then checking it against our own experience. So there is a need often to delve behind his words. As he often said, "The word is not the thing."

The impression one often gets is that he wants to jolt our brains out of a complacent sluggishness that we have wrongly taken for granted, as though we are unwitting prisoners of limitations that we fail to see are self-imposed. Again, for him this is the kind of issue that can only be explored by each one of us, and no one else has the right to answer on our behalf.

At a talk in India in 1965, after Krishnamurti had spoken of the need for radical, deep change in the human being, a member of the audience protested, "We are all ordinary human beings." His response was, "We cannot afford to be ordinary human beings anymore . . . the challenge is too immense." At another talk a member of the audience argued that none of the great religious teachers had fundamentally changed the world, and neither would Krishnamurti. His answer: "Our problem is, can we immediately and altogether stop thinking in terms of becoming? That is the only new approach." Perhaps it is worth explaining for new readers that preoccupation with becoming something or somebody was for Krishnamurti the major hurdle to understanding one's present state of being, which he called *what is*. And an ongoing understanding of that, he proposed, was the key to understanding not just one's own consciousness but human consciousness as a whole, and much more besides.

So was the problem he raised solvable? He maintained that it was if one was tremendously interested, faced a new problem afresh, and gave one's heart and mind to it. The expression "throwing down the gauntlet" springs to mind.

PART TWO of this book contains, edited and slightly abridged, the last four talks and two question-and-answer sessions Krishnamurti gave in England in 1985, the year before he died at the age of ninety-one. He had talked for more than fifty years around the world, and, though this was not known at the time, these talks were to be a farewell address to his audience in Europe. Is this a summing-up, or final testimony to a never-ending inquiry? He did raise perhaps the most fundamental question of all by asking what is the origin of creation, of all things—and the reader may find what he says on that topic surprising. His style is simpler and more direct; his subject matter contains variations on themes echoed throughout his talks in previous decades, but as usual it also contains points that are fresh and new. Whatever the gravity of the challenge he saw facing humanity, he was alive as ever to the beauty of the earth, to life as the supreme teacher, to life as immensity.

Krishnamurti spoke often of the need to live seriously but also of the inseparability of learning and enjoyment: "I have learned hapily what my attachments do to the mind." "What do you mean by the word *consciousness*? It is fun if you go into all this." "To me it is very enjoyable, if I may use that word, to find out why my mind is attached to property." For him, to detect an illusion and unravel a misperception seems to be like the delight a mathematician feels in solving an equation. Perhaps this conveys a message that some kind of natural unfolding of awareness, an endless learning—which we may unknowingly be obstructing—is what it means to be truly alive.

DAVID SKITT

# PART ONE

# I ✺ STANDING ALONE

I WONDER WHY YOU HAVE COME. Is it curiosity, or do you have problems you want someone else to solve, or are you seriously concerned about what is happening in the world and, being serious, desire earnestly to solve the appalling, frightening problems that surround us? So is it curiosity, or wanting your personal problems solved, or because you see the extraordinary events in the world—the sorrow, the violence, the division of nationalities, the political and religious divisions, and all the separative issues? One must, it seems to me, be very clear about this.

For my part, I want to say something very clearly and definitely. I have spoken for fifty years, all over the world, except in Russia and China, and in observing all these years the state of the world, the state of human beings and their relationships with each other, one sees very clearly that the problem is not only external but much more deeply inward. And without solving the complex, inward issues, merely to be concerned with the outward phenomena has very little significance. I feel, observing all this, that one must take a totally different action, enter into a totally different dimension, not belong to any organized religion, or any country, any political movement, be totally uncommitted so that one can look clearly, objectively, sanely at all the phenomena that are going on around us and within us.

If you are serious, and I hope you are, then we have a relationship with each other, otherwise we have none whatsoever. That is clear, isn't it? If you and I are both serious about understanding this whole phenomenon of existence, not only outwardly but also much more deeply inwardly, and are totally concerned with the resolution of this problem, then you and I have a relationship; then we can move together, think together, share together. And sharing, thinking, investigating together, and therefore creating together, is communication.

I hope I am making myself clear. We cannot communicate with each other if you are interested merely in trying to solve a particular little problem of your own, which we may deal with later, or if you are merely curious to know what this chap from India with his strange philosophy has to say, or are interested in some exotic nonsense. Then I am afraid you and I will not communicate. Because the speaker is not bringing or talking about any particular system of philosophy—and the real meaning of philosophy is the understanding of truth in daily life, in daily action, which has nothing whatsoever to do with Christianity, with Buddhism, with Hinduism, or with any particular culture.

So if we are really very earnest, and the time demands that we be so, then we must see very clearly, objectively, nonpersonally this whole world as it is—divided, broken up by nationalities, by religious beliefs, or by the sectarian beliefs of politics, the various ideologies, each fighting the other and trying to bring about a unity while keeping itself separate. There are wars, there is all this political chicanery, and the slow pace of bringing human beings together through politics. You know all this. Yet I wonder if you are aware of it intellectually, verbally, or if you are aware of it with your heart, with your whole mind.

So one has to first find out for oneself how deeply one is

aware of this division between human beings through nationalities, through religious beliefs, through belonging to this or that sect, following this or that guru, this or that system—they are all divisions. And through division there can never be the unity of humankind. Now, how deeply is one aware of this phenomenon? Intellectually, one may admit that it exists, and assert it verbally, but does one *feel* this extraordinary division between human beings, between a wife and a husband, between friends, the division of color, race, class, and so on? How deeply is one aware of it? And if one is aware of it in the normal sense of that word—which is to be concerned, to know all the implications of this division—then what is one to do?

What is a human being, you, to do in a world that is so divided? The outer and the inner, the conscious and the unconscious, the rich and the poor, the learned and the ignorant, the technician and the layman, the artist, the businessman, the hippie, the long-haired and the short-haired, this whole division. If one is aware of it, what is one to do? Do you ask that question casually, assuming that this division will eventually end some thousand years in the future and therefore depends on the outer environment, certain political systems, and so on? Or it is a problem that demands your immediate attention and action, which means you are intense about it, you want to solve it with your whole being? That is why we asked what interests you. Are you aware of this division between human beings, which has existed for thousands and thousands of years not only outwardly but each one divided in himself, in conflict in himself, fighting in himself, battling to become, to be, to fulfill, to assert, to dominate?

So there is this question: What is one to do, how is one to act? By a collective response, or by a response that comes from the freedom of a human being, and then in that freedom to act collectively? We must act collectively because great changes are demanded, but it is deep psychological revolution that is necessary, not mere physical revolution, not throwing bombs and killing thousands of people in the name of order, of a new society, in the name of peace. That there must be such a deep psychological revolution is not a dogmatic statement on the speaker's part; it is what is demanded, it is what one observes to be necessary. Is that revolution to be brought about by collective action? That is, through different types of education, forcing the individual, the human being, through conditioning to behave properly? This is what is being done, and therefore denying total freedom to the human being, though it may bring about a collective action. Or is the revolution to free the mind from conditioning, and in that freedom to bring about a cooperative action? Am I making myself clear?

So we are not emphasizing the individual or the collective, because the world is divided in that way; neither are we emphasizing the freedom of the individual, and therefore allowing him to do what he likes, nor emphasizing collective action that will drown the individual. We are talking about something entirely different, neither this nor that.

You see, human beings are so disorderly, so self-concerned, so utterly selfish that religions throughout the world with their beliefs, dogmas, rituals, saviors, and all the rest of that circus have tried to condition them to behave through fear. You can see it in Christianity, in Buddhism, in every kind of organized religion—condition human minds through fear. And modern psychologists, from what they have told me, are trying to condition the human being not through punishment but through reward. It is the same thing, two sides of the same coin. Because the human being must behave, become sane, orderly, have right relationship with others, whether black, brown, colored, or whatever it is. And as human beings apparently cannot behave, therefore they impose authority, conditioning through fear and reward, or offering physical or psychological security. Are you following all this?

May I go on? I'll go on anyhow because it interests me tremendously, because we must create a different kind of people, a different kind of human mind, which doesn't belong to the past, which is neither of the left nor right, which is entirely different.

So seeing all this, there must be a collective action in which the human being is totally free, and the question is whether that freedom can bring about harmony in relationship and therefore in behavior. So that is our problem: how a human mind, your mind, which has been so conditioned by the past, through the present to the future, how can such a mind be changed radically? Then the question is whether it will take time, time being gradual, taking several years, or as the Asiatics say, several lives, which is the same thing. Or is it to be brought about by instant perception? That is, suppose my mind is conditioned as a Catholic, Buddhist, Communist, whatever it is. I realize that it is conditioned, not as an idea or as a speculative formula, but I realize that it actually is conditioned. Now, will it change through analysis, analytical processes, or through pressure, which is reward and punishment, or is there a totally different approach to this problem?

Please, you are sharing this; you are not just listening to me. If you just listen to it casually, accepting certain words and denying others, or agreeing or disagreeing, it will be of little significance. Whereas if you share in this, so we actually communicate with each other, then you will have to find out for yourself whether time is involved in this problem—time being a long period that you have to go through analytically, either by yourself or through another, or you are compelled by circumstances and environment to bring about change, all of which implies time. Or, as I have said, is there a totally different approach to this question?

Now, what do you think? How do you look at this problem? Because we are sharing, exploring this together. The speaker is not an authority, not your beastly guru, nor are you his followers. We are human beings trying to resolve this immense problem of existence. So if you are serious, we have to share this thing together. Therefore you have to listen, not only to what is said but also to your own reactions, your own thoughts and feelings. You have this problem before you: It has been said that you cannot possibly change the human mind instantly, that time is needed to gradually bring about this radical, psychological revolution. That has been said in the past and in the present. This has been the philosophy, the attitude, the assertion: You cannot change the human mind—which has been so conditioned—instantly.

Let us look at this idea. It really is an idea, you follow, a formula that the human mind cannot be instantly and radically changed psychologically, and that it must have time. That is a concept, a supposition, a theory. Now, the root meaning of that word *theory* is to behold, to have an insight. Now, follow that. You have an insight into something, then from that insight you formulate an idea, a concept, and act according to that concept.

So how is a mind like ours that is so heavily conditioned, whether we acknowledge this or not, both consciously and deeply—the conditioning being the past, whether that is yesterday or a thousand yesterdays—how is that mind to free itself from its conditioning so that it is free to behave properly, to establish true relationship with another in which there is love and not division? You have understood the problem, I hope, so how do you set about it? What is the truth of this? Not according to any psychologist, whether ancient or modern, not according to any religious teacher—wipe all that away, if you can, and look at it. Can you wipe out your associations with any group, with any particular system, with any particular ideology? Perhaps you can't. To wipe out means to stand completely alone. Then you can face the problem. Are you doing this?

To stand alone in the world is one of the most difficult things:

not to belong to any nation, except perhaps having a passport; not to belong to any ideology, any particular kind of activity of the left or right; not to repeat a single word that you yourself have not known, so that there is integrity. Because if you belong to any organization, any group, or follow any guru, anyone, you are not being honest. So, in a world that is so disorderly, divided, full of antagonism, bitterness, and falsehood, can you stand completely alone? Sorry, either you do this or you don't. You can't say, "Well, I do belong to a particular little group, but I am really free from all that." You know, when there is no integrity, when there is no honesty and virtue, systems and organizations become tremendously important. Haven't you noticed this? Then the organizations, systems, control the mind. But if the mind is really honest, straight, clear, then no system is required because it is totally virtuous. I wonder if you follow all this?

So we are faced with this problem: How is a mind that is so controlled, shaped by environment, conditioned by various influences, by the education that one has, by competition, aggression, violence, all that—how is such a mind to free itself, so that it is *totally* free and sane? Now, how would you, who are also very intellectual, who have read so much, solve this problem? Would you rely on someone else to solve it? That means on authority, right? Whether the authority of the analyst, the psychologist, the priest, or the authority of a savior, you know the whole business—would you put your faith, belief, in somebody else to solve this problem for you?

Go on, answer it for yourself. You see, unfortunately, we do rely on someone else, because we say, "I don't know, I don't know how to solve this problem. It is too complex. I haven't given enough time to it, I haven't really thought about it. And somebody has given time, gone into it greatly, and I will accept what he says." And you add, "Why not? He knows, I don't." So you make him into the authority and are therefore living a secondhand life. And this is not a secondhand issue, it is your issue; *you* have to solve it, not through somebody else, not by having faith in something. We have played that game for thousands of years with our gurus, our saviors, our masters, our professionals, and we haven't changed. So it is your problem, therefore you cannot possibly rely on anybody, especially on the speaker. Right? The speaker means me!

So can you discard what another says you should think or do, and come face to face with yourself, directly and firsthand? Then you put aside all authority, except the authority of law, which says keep to the right of the road and pay tax. I am not talking about that kind of authority, but the authority on which you depend for your beliefs, in which you have faith, when you acknowledge that someone else knows more than you do about yourself. So this brings you totally to yourself, and therefore you have tremendous energy. Because I waste energy in listening to somebody else, following somebody else, putting my faith in something, whether in a society, a community, a person, an idea, or some system. That is a waste of energy. Whereas when I totally discard dependence on another for my behavior, my integrity, my honesty, my sanity, then I have tremendous energy to look at what I am. Are you doing it? Do it. Then it is fun discussing with you.

So now we are asking, Can this mind that has been conditioned both superficially and also deeply unconsciously, the totality of it, can that be radically transformed? If you put that question seriously to yourself, then you and I have a relationship in investigating the question. You are not taking sides. It is you who are investigating, not through the eyes of somebody else. Now, how does one investigate? I cannot investigate it if I want to get through it to reach an end. If I say that I will investigate it to find a different state, in order to be free, then it is not investigation. You have already started with a motive, and that motive is going to direct your investigation.

So the mind must be free of all motive in order to investigate. Are you doing this? Because one sees so much suffering in the world, the poor, the starving, people who live in ghettos in the overpopulated, underdeveloped countries, where poverty is a curse, where there is so much physical illness. And there are other kinds of suffering—suffering created by the human being in his divisiveness, the wars. You know this sorrow, don't you? One sees this, feels it, one is aware of it, both the inward sorrow as well as the outward sorrow. And one has to respond, one has to solve it; one can't just say, well, it is part of existence, it is inevitable in human nature and so on. You have to solve it, you have to go beyond it. And we have the intelligence to do that. But that intelligence comes into being only when you don't depend on anybody, when you are face to face with yourself and with the problem. Intelligence is, after all, the capacity of total energy in application.

So now I have the energy, because I don't depend on anyone. Can you honestly, seriously say that you don't depend on anybody, on your friend, your environment, your guru, your book? That you don't have faith in something or a belief in something? This doesn't mean that you become agnostic or all that silly stuff. You are a human being completely with yourself, resolving the human problem of existence, and not therefore having somebody else resolving your problems.

As we have said, investigation demands energy, energy that is the application of intelligence, and intelligence cannot be if you are looking to another. He may be intelligent, but if you look to him you are ignorant. Now, how do you investigate? Who is the investigator? It is no good saying to oneself, "I am going to investigate" without trying to find out who the investigator is. Sorry, is this becoming too complex?

Say I want to investigate this problem of the mind, which is "me," my mind: why it is conditioned, how deeply it is conditioned, and whether it can be wholly free from that conditioning.

Only then can I have a right relationship with another human being, because my conditioning divides me and brings about a division between you and me. My image of "me" is the dividing factor. So I must first find out who the investigator is. Is it one of the many fragments of the "me" that is investigating—one part, one fragment saying, "I will investigate the different fragments," which is the "me" that is conditioned? So one part assumes the authority and capacity to investigate the other parts. One part is broken up and against the other parts. So is that investigation when one part assumes the authority to investigate the other fragments?

That is not investigation. It is a conclusion that says, "I will investigate." Do you see this? It is a conclusion. And that conclusion brings about a division. So to investigate there must be no conclusion, no hypothesis. The meaning of *hypothesis* is foundation, and if you start from a foundation, which is inevitably a conclusion, and investigate with that conclusion, it brings about a division, and therefore it is not an investigation. If you see this clearly, you will proceed further.

So is my mind, which is investigating, free from a conclusion? Which is: "I will investigate." A conclusion is the expression of will, right? When I say, "I will investigate myself," it is a conclusion brought about by my desire to understand, to go beyond in order to reach a certain dimension in which all the present misery doesn't exist. It is a conclusion. It is the action of will that says, "I will investigate." So can my mind be free of that conclusion? Otherwise I cannot investigate. It is like a scientist: If he wants to investigate, he looks. He doesn't start with a conclusion—then he is not a scientist, he is just a . . . I don't know what he is!

So to investigate, to inquire, is to be free of any conclusion. Then the mind is clear, fresh. And then when you proceed, is there an investigator at all? Then there is only *observation*, not investigation. Therefore such a mind is not broken up, and only then is it capable of observing. Observing, which means having insight without a conclusion, and therefore continuous insight. Are you getting all this? So the mind is free to observe and therefore to act totally.

Would you like to ask any questions? I am sorry to force you all to observe!

QUESTIONER: Can you state more clearly your attitude toward psychoanalysis and neurosis?

KRISHNAMURTI: I wonder how many of us are neurotic—which means not sane. Obviously any man who belongs to any nationality, or who follows any guru or authority, is not sane. Right? The word *sanity* means whole, healthy. How can a mind that is healthy belong to any group, to any tribe, which is the essence of nationalism, or follow anybody? So when one says, "Who is neurotic?" I am afraid most of us are.

And the questioner asks, Would you please explain more clearly your attitude toward psychoanalysis? Are you interested in this? I don't know why people get analyzed. When the analyst himself is so terribly conditioned, why should you put yourself in his hands? When you yourself are conditioned, more or less slightly unbalanced, that is up to you; why should you hand yourself over to a conditioned analyst? You know what he is— he is conditioned according to his studies, his Jung or Freud, this, that, and the other, and also he is conditioned by his own worries, his own family, his relationships, his position in society, and all that.

The dictionary meaning of the word *analysis* is to break up. And we are broken-up human beings, we are contradictory; there is self-contradiction in us; we are different fragments, we are happy, unhappy, dishonest, honest, we hate. And analysis implies either the outside analyzer, the professional, or the inward analyzer who is yourself. If I analyze myself, I have to find out who the analyzer is before I trot out the analysis. Who am I that is going to analyze myself? Who am I? I say, "I'll examine myself, why I behave this way or that, why I do this or that." One part of me examines. And so that part brings about a division among the parts. Now, is there analysis if there are no parts? Of course not. So my concern is not analysis but to see if there is a possibility of bringing about total harmony. And this cannot be brought about by integration, that is, by adding the broken parts to make a whole. And who is it who adds? We come back to the same thing.

So to me analysis is a waste of time because I can go on analyzing myself to the end of my days, creating conflict in myself by saying this is right, this is wrong; beating myself sick, which is neurotic. Whereas my question is, Can I see, observe, wholly without division? And to observe wholly is sanity. So I must watch how my mind is operating, watch, observe, not correct it, not shape it, not say, "I must be whole, I must be sane"—which is insane—but watch. So it depends how the mind watches. Does it watch with a conclusion, with condemnation, with judgment, with evaluation, with previous memories? The mind can watch only when it is completely free to observe. And you do that if you have tremendous interest and vitality.

# 2 🌀 LIVING CREATIVELY

WE HAVE SAID HOW IMPORTANT it is that, seeing how inevitably corrupt the various types of religious, secular, and social organizations are, to belong to any of them not only prevents the unburdening of one's conditioning but also prevents one from seeing things clearly. We have said that it is important to be able to stand completely alone, not adhering to any group or sect, following any teacher or guru, so that we can bring about quite a different kind of society. I do not know if you see the importance of or have an insight into this question, because most of us are very confused. There are so many demands and pressures that most of us lean on somebody—we want to be guided and told what to do. In ourselves we have no clarity, and of course there are those who say that they are very clear, in a state of enlightenment, or of freedom, and so on. And being uncertain ourselves, we more or less yield to their persuasion and so not only become more conditioned but accept a new form of conditioning. And if we are conditioned in this way, our mind inevitably becomes almost mechanical.

Please, as we have also said, we are sharing this thing together, thinking over these problems together and therefore understanding them together. It is not that I am telling you what to think or how to think, but rather that we together investigate, understand, have an insight into all these problems, so that you are very clear at the end of it. So that in that clarity you stand alone. Because one must bring about a totally different kind of society, a totally different kind of human being, and the more one sees what is happening in the world, the greater the demand for such a human being.

It is only the mind that is capable of standing alone—in the sense of not belonging to any group, any party, any community, any set of dogmas, beliefs, conclusions—that can be creative. So I think we have to go into the question of what it is to be creative, because if that is not clear we are apt to follow those things that make the mind more and more mechanical, dependent, and attached. So what is it to be creative? Because if you are not creative, you will inevitably be fragmented, accept authority, succumb to all the absurdities of escapes. I do not know what the word *creative* means to you. It is not, surely, creating some new kind of physical thing—a new invention, a new mode of speech, of painting, or of music. We are talking of a mind that is standing alone and therefore capable of being creative.

Most of us are in conflict, caught in various kinds of demands, not only physical but environmental, social, and so on. We depend on each other both physically and psychologically, and therefore our whole nature, our psychological structure, is fragmented. Please observe it in yourself. Can a mind that is fragmented, contradictory in itself, be creative? Or does creation take place when there is the absence of the continuity of fragmentation? I don't know if you follow all this. Does it interest you? Because if we are not creative in the deeper sense of that word, into which we are going, we are bound to escape from the central fact of deep frustration. And the escapes then become very important, whether they are religious, political, sexual escapes, or escapes into good works. So the escapes become all-important, and not the factor of this fragmentation in which a mind is caught. Please do follow this. And observing this in oneself—how one is fragmented, contradictory, being pulled by different desires, demands—how is a mind to be free, in which alone there can be creation?

First of all, do you know what it means, what takes place, when you have an insight into something? Say, for instance, you have an insight into the whole business of organized religion; you see what is implied in it, how corrupt, how false it is. You can have such insight only when the mind is not conditioned, not attached to any particular form of belief, right? Now, having an insight into the religious structure, you then draw a conclusion from that. But when you draw that conclusion, you terminate that insight. You put an end to it by drawing a conclusion from it. Is that clear?

I must make this very clear so that you understand it. I see very clearly what it means to belong to any political party, which must be nationalistic, run by people who are utterly corrupt, working for themselves in the name of the party, wanting power, position, and all the rest of it. I have an insight into that, not through book knowledge, not through reading, but actually through seeing it. From that perception I draw a conclusion that politicians, all politics, are dreadful. Now, by drawing a conclusion from it, I have terminated that insight. You follow? So I act from the conclusion and not from that insight. So my action from a conclusion is mechanical, and being mechanical I then say, "How terrible to live mechanically. I want to escape." I join a community, I become whatever I do, escaping from the mechanical process of living, which is the result of a conclusion from an insight I had into something.

You see the sequence of it? So when I act on a conclusion, my action must be continuously mechanical, though at the beginning

I may have had an insight. Now, if one doesn't draw a conclusion at all, and there is only insight, then action is nonmechanical. Therefore that action is always creative, always new, always living. So a mind that has insight and acts from that without drawing a conclusion is in the movement of continuous, constant insight. Do you understand this? Understand, not verbally, but actually *see* the truth of this, as you see the truth of a precipice?

Now, this constant insight without a formula, a conclusion that puts an end to that insight, is creative action—have you got it? Please look at it, go into it yourself. It is astonishingly beautiful and interesting how thought is absent when you have an insight. Thought cannot have an insight. It is only when the mind is not operating mechanically in the structure of thought that you have an insight. When you have an insight, thought draws a conclusion from that insight. And then thought acts, and thought is mechanical. Are we following each other? So I have to find out whether in having an insight into myself—which means into the world, myself being the world and the world is me—there is no drawing of a conclusion from it. If I draw a conclusion, I act on an idea, on an image, on a symbol that is the structure of thought, and so I am constantly preventing myself from having insight, preventing myself from understanding things as they are. So I have to go into this whole question of why thought interferes and draws a conclusion when there is a perception. Have you understood my question?

I perceive something to be true, I perceive that to control oneself—listen to this carefully—brings about a division in myself between the controller and the controlled and therefore conflict. I have an insight into that, that is the truth, but my whole thinking process is conditioned to the idea that I must control. My education, my religion, the society in which I live, the family structure, everything says to me "control," which is the conclusion that has been handed down to me, the conclusion that I have also acquired, and I act according to that conclusion, which is mechanical. And therefore I live in constant strife.

Now I have an insight into this whole problem of control, an insight that came into being when the mind was free to observe, unconditioned. But this whole structure of conditioning still remains. So now there is a mind that says, "By Jove, I have seen this thing very clearly, but I am also caught in the habit of control." So there is a battle. One thing is mechanical, the other is non-mechanical. Now, why does thought cling to the whole structure of control? Because thought has brought about this idea of control. Do you see this?

What does it mean to control? First, it implies suppression. Division in oneself, with one part, one segment of me saying, "I must control the other segments." That division is created by thought. Thought says, "I must control myself because otherwise I would not adapt myself to the environment, to what people say, and so forth, so therefore I must control." So thought, being the response of memory—which means the past, one's experience, one's knowledge, which are all mechanical—has immense power. So there is constant battle between perception, insight, and conditioning.

Now what is the mind to do? This is our problem. You see something new, but the old is still there—the old habits, ideas, beliefs, all that is tremendously waiting. So how is the mind to sustain an insight without ever having a conclusion? Because if I have a conclusion, it is mechanical, the result of thought, the result of memory. From memory there is a reaction as thought. Then it becomes mechanical, then it becomes old. Now, please experiment with me.

There is insight—seeing something new, seeing something that is totally new, clear, beautiful—and there is the past with all the memory, experience, knowledge, and from that there is thought that is cautious, watching, afraid, concerned about how to bring the new into the old. Now, when you see this problem clearly, what takes place? Have you understood my question? We are the result of the past. The younger generation may try to break away from the past, and think they are free to create a new world, but they are not free from the past. They are reacting to the past and therefore continuing with the past. I don't know if you follow this. So there is not a break with the past but a modified continuity of the past.

So I see this: I see what thought has done, and also there is clear perception that insight exists only when there is absence of thought. Now, how do you solve this problem? Perhaps you are thinking about it, looking at it for the first time. So how do you respond to this? How does the mind respond to this?

Let me put the question differently. Mind must have knowledge: I must know where I live. Mind must know the language it speaks. It must exercise thought—thought that is the response of memory, experience, knowledge, which is the past. Otherwise there would be no communication between you and me; I wouldn't know where I lived and all the rest of it, and absurdities begin if I am not capable of thinking clearly. So I see knowledge is necessary to function in the mechanical world. Going from here to the place I live is mechanical, speaking a language is mechanical, acting from knowledge is mechanical, acting from all kinds of experience is mechanical. And that mechanical process must to a certain extent continue. Like my insight. Have you got it? So when there is insight there is no contradiction between knowledge and freedom from knowledge.

So there is the insight now that knowledge is necessary, and there is also the insight that comes when there is the absence of thought. So there is perception, insight, all the time, not a contradiction. I wonder if you see this?

See the difficulty in putting into words what I want to convey. I want to convey to you that a mind that is constantly operating

upon a conclusion inevitably becomes mechanical, and being mechanical it must escape into some kind of illusion, some kind of
mythology, some kind of religious circus. And you have an insight into that. You say, "By Jove, how true that is." Now, if you
draw a conclusion from that insight, you have moved to a different place, but it is still mechanical. I don't know if you see this.
So when you have constant insight *without a conclusion*, that state of
mind is creative—not the mind that is in conflict, and through
conflict produces pictures or books. Not the mind that is in conflict—it can never be creative. Now, if you see that, that is an insight, isn't it? You can see it, we'll take it up.

You know in the world of art and literature, people say, "He
is a great artist, he is a great creative writer." But if you look behind the literature to the author, you will see that he is in daily
conflict—with his wife, with his family, with society; he is ambitious, he is greedy, he wants power, position, prestige. And he
has certain talents for writing. Through tensions, through conflict, he may write very good books, but he is not creative in the
deep sense of the word. And we are trying to see if each one of
us can be creative in that deep sense, not in expression, that is, in
writing a book, a poem, or whatever it is, but having insight and
never drawing a conclusion from that insight, so that you are
moving constantly from insight to insight, action to action.
That is spontaneity.

Now, such a mind must obviously be alone—but not in the
sense of being isolated. What is the difference between isolation
and being alone? I am isolated when I build a wall of resistance
around myself. I resist, I resist any criticism, any new idea; I am
afraid, I want to protect myself, I don't want to be hurt. And so
that brings about in my action a self-centered activity that is an
isolating process. And most of us are isolating ourselves. I have
been hurt and I don't want to be hurt. The memory of that hurt
remains, and therefore I resist. Or I believe in Jesus or Krishna,

or whatever it is, and I resist any suggestion of doubt, anything criticizing my belief, because I have taken security in my belief. That isolates. That isolation may be thousands of people, millions of people, but it is still isolation. When I say I am a Catholic, or a Communist, or whatever it is, I am isolating myself. And aloneness is entirely different. It is not the opposite of isolation, but—listen to this carefully—when there is insight into isolation, that insight is aloneness. Have you got it?

So, I do not know if you have noticed—we will go into this much more deeply on a different occasion—that death is the final state of complete isolation. You are leaving everything behind, all your works, your ideas, you are completely isolated through fear of that thing. And that isolation is wholly different from understanding the whole nature of death. If you have an insight into that, you are alone. I wonder if you are getting this? I see you are not. Leave it for the moment; we'll come back to it.

So a mind that is free has insight every minute. A mind that is free has no conclusion and is therefore nonmechanical. Such a mind is in action, nonmechanical action, because it sees the fact that there is insight into everything each minute. So it is constantly moving, alive, and therefore such a mind is always young, fresh, and incapable of being hurt, whereas the mechanical mind is capable of being hurt.

So thought, upon which all our civilizations are based, becomes mechanical. And all our civilizations are mechanical and therefore corrupt. I don't know if you are following all this. Therefore, to belong to any organization is to become corrupt, or to allow oneself to be corrupted. Now, that is an insight, isn't it? Can you then move from that insight to another insight and keep moving, which is living, and therefore relationship becomes a totally different thing? Because our relationships are based on conclusions, aren't they? Do watch this, please do have an insight into this, and you will see how extraordinary a change takes place in your relationships if you really have insight into this.

First of all, our relationship is mechanical, which means it is based on ideas, on a conclusion, on images, isn't it? I have an image about my wife, or she has an image about me—image in the sense of knowledge, a conclusion, experience—and from that conclusion, knowledge, image, she acts, and she adds to that image, conclusion, through action, just as the other, the man does. So the relationship is between two conclusions. I don't know if you see this. And therefore the relationship is mechanical. You may call it love, you may sleep together, but it is mechanical. Because it is mechanical, you then want excitement—religious excitement, psychological excitement, and every form of entertainment—to escape from this mechanical relationship. You divorce and try to find another woman or man who will have something new, but that also soon becomes mechanical.

So our relationships are based on this mechanical process. Now, if you have an insight into this, see it as actually it is—the pleasure, the so-called love, the so-called antagonism, the frustrations, the images, conclusions that you have built about her and about yourself—if you have an insight into that, it all disappears, doesn't it? You no longer have an image, which is a conclusion. I wonder if you are following all this? So your relationship is direct, not through an image. And our relationship is based on thought, on the intellect, which is mechanical, and that has obviously nothing whatsoever to do with love. I may say, "I love my wife," but it is not an actual fact. I love the image that I have about her when she is not attacking me. So I now discover that relationship means freedom from image, from conclusion, and relationship therefore means responsibility and love. You follow? Which is not a conclusion, you understand?

So my brain is the storehouse of knowledge, various experiences and memories, hurts, images, which is thought. Right? Do see this. And my brain, which is yours as well as mine, my brain is conditioned through time, through evolution, through growth. And its function is to live in complete security, naturally, otherwise it can't function, and so it builds a wall around itself as belief, dogma, prestige, power, position—it builds all that around itself as a means to be completely secure. I don't know if you have followed all this? Have you watched your own brain operating? You will find that it can function remarkably well, logically, sanely, when it is not frightened. That means when it has complete security.

Now, is there complete security? So, feeling uncertain without complete security, it then proceeds to conclude that there is security. It makes a conclusion. So conclusion becomes its security, right? Is this too much? Are you following all this? Look, say I am frightened, and I see I can only function, the brain can only function, when there is really happy, enjoyable security. But there isn't such security because I am frightened—I may lose my job, my wife, whatever. You follow? I am frightened. And so through fear I invest my energy in a belief, in a conclusion that becomes my security. That belief, that conclusion, may be an illusion, a myth, a nonsense, but it is my security. I believe in all the business of churches and all that; it is an absolute myth, but that is my security. So I find security in a belief, or in a neurotic behavior—because to behave neurotically is also a form of security.

So the brain can only function freely and fully in complete security. It must have security, whether it is real or false, illusory or nonexistent, and so it will invent some form of security. Now I see that there is no security in belief, in a conclusion, in any person, in any social structure, in any leader, in following anybody. I see that there is no security in that, right? So I have security in seeing, in having insight. I wonder if you see this? *There is security in insight, not in conclusion.* Have you got it? Not from me, but for yourself, have you captured it, is it real to you?

So we have this problem, this problem of a mind, of the brain, that can function only in complete order, in complete security, in complete certainty, otherwise it gets deranged, neurotic. Therefore I see that putting one's faith in any person, myself included, in any leader, in any organization, is a neurotic action. So what is the security that a mind has when it has discarded all this? Its security is in insight, which brings intelligence. Have you got it? Security is in intelligence. Not in knowledge, not in experience, but in insight into the value of knowledge, and therefore that insight is the capacity of sustained intelligence, and in that there is security. Therefore that intelligence, that insight, is never frightened. Do you get it?

It would be a tremendous thing if we could, all of us together, understand this one thing: the nature of awareness, of perception, and of insight. You understand? Because then the mind is free to live. To live, not to live in conflict, in battle, in suspicion, in fear, being hurt, and all the rest of that misery.

QUESTIONER: Today we hear about the new Jesus wave acting in the world, for instance, in the United States among young people. Is there a spiritual power, Christ, at present acting on this earth?

KRISHNAMURTI: If I live in a remote Indian village, I will never have heard of Jesus, will I? I wouldn't know anything about Jesus, but I would know about my particular Jesus, Krishna. Or some other deity I have been brought up with. People who have been conditioned by two thousand years of the mythology of Jesus break away from it and come back to it. Have you noticed this? You give up Jesus for a year, or a couple of years, and pick it up again. You become a Communist or a Socialist, then drop it and go back to church or join a new cult. So look at it carefully, have an insight into this.

The whole Western world is conditioned by a religious concept that is based on idea, on thought, on a personal worship of the savior. In India, in Asia, they are similarly conditioned, but by a different series of images, ideas, and conclusions. Probably they have never heard of Jesus. In a Buddhist country they don't even consider Jesus. So there are different parts of the world conditioned by religious concepts. Right? And the questioner asks, Is there a new spiritual awakening, a new spiritual wave? Obviously the wave of the Indian concept of religion, or of the Christian concept, Jesus, is not a new wave at all. It is the continuity of the old conditioned responses acting differently, but they are still conditioned responses.

Let me put it differently. When the speaker goes to India, there are various gurus with immense followings, and the followers say, "This is a new wave, a new spiritual awakening." And because they follow their old guru it is not new, it is just a repetition of the old in a different form. So this is happening right through the world: the repetition of a religiously conditioned mind, acting or not acting in a different way. To me, personally, that is not a spiritual awakening at all. Obviously it can't be. If I become a Hindu, or I am a Hindu, I do all the circus involved in Hinduism; there is nothing new in it, I am going back to repeating the old stuff. The newness lies in freedom, you understand? In freedom from being conditioned, so that I am neither a Christian, a Buddhist, a Hindu, nor a Muslim.

Because the mind must be free to find out what truth is. It cannot be free if it accepts the authority of any church, any savior, or any book. And a new spiritual awakening is possible only when there are some in the world, whether a few or many, who have really gone into this whole problem deeply, who have freed themselves completely and stand completely alone. Because it is only when people are alone, when the human mind is alone, that it is possible to have real relationship with others. And it is only such a mind that can find out, can come upon that thing that is beyond time, beyond measure. That is the real awakening, something totally new taking place. And that is your responsibility. Not just sitting here and listening to a speaker, agreeing or disagreeing, accepting a few ideas. It is your responsibility to see that you, as a human being, are free from your conditioning, stand alone, and therefore live in integrity, honesty, and virtue—and that is the new.

Q: How is the mind to cease being limited and mechanical?

K: Our minds are automatic, limited, small, mechanical. How am I, the questioner asks, to be free of this? I have just explained this. But all right, let's go into it.

My mind is petty, mechanical, small—what am I to do with it? Do you know your mind is small, petty, anxious, jealous, envious, competitive, comparing? Do you? Are you aware of your mind being like that? Oh, for God's sake, let's be honest sometime. Right. I am aware of it. What shall I do?

So when you say, "I am aware of it," what do you mean by that word *aware*? When you say, "I know my mind is petty," what do you mean by that word *know*? Please, this is important. Do you know it because you have compared your mind with another mind that is not petty? I say, "My mind is petty, narrow, stupid, dull, idiotic, neurotic." How do I know that? Because somebody has told me? Because I have compared it with another mind that I think is not neurotic, that I think is free? So do I discover my pettiness through comparison, through measurement? Now, measurement, comparison, is the factor that makes the mind petty. I don't know if you see this. Now, this is an insight. You understand? I compare, I measure myself with you who are very clever, bright, clear-eyed, and nice-looking, and I say, "Oh my God, how dull I am!"

What does that mean? Through comparison I have found that I am dull. This is my education. I have been educated to always compare myself—in school, in college, as I grow up—to measure myself against another. So I say to myself, Why do I measure at all? If I don't measure, am I dull? I don't know. I have assumed through comparison that I am dull. Please follow this. This is an insight. And can the mind that is conditioned through centuries of education to compare religiously, economically, socially, in every way to compare, to measure—can that measurement come to an end? That is my first question. It can only come to an end if I have an insight into the stupidity of measurement.

Why should I compare myself with you? You may be the most marvelous human being, the greatest saint on earth, or the savior, but why should I compare myself with you? I do this because I have been educated to do it—my brother is better than me, my uncle is much brighter than me. So I have an insight that says, Don't compare, that is silly. Now, having had an insight into that, I stop comparing. Then what am I? You follow? What am I? I don't know, I really don't know. Are you following this? When you don't compare yourself with somebody, what are you?

You are going to find out, aren't you? You don't say, "I am petty, small, bourgeois, limited, how ugly." I don't know what I am. So I am going to find out. When I say, "I am stupid, dull, narrow," I have come to a conclusion through comparison. A conclusion puts an end to insight. So the insight shows me the futility of comparison. I won't compare. It is finished, forever. Therefore I am going to see what I am. The moment I reject comparison, I am no longer stupid because I have an insight into the whole structure of comparison, which is intelligence, which is greater than the value of comparing pettiness and greatness. Have you got it?

# 3 ❀ IMAGES MADE BY THOUGHT DESTROY HUMAN RELATIONSHIP

I WOULD LIKE TO TALK about something that is perhaps life's most fundamental problem. And we should understand it not merely verbally but also go beyond the words and have a deep insight into what is being said. I can talk about it for an hour or more because I have gone into it pretty thoroughly in myself, but I would like, if I may, to share with you what I think is really important. The word *share* means to share the beauty of a tree together, to look at a river, see together all the movement, the color, the shadows. And sharing implies a responsibility that you and I, both of us, partake in when we look at a mountain and have that sense of extraordinary beauty, great height, nobility, and majesty. And sharing can take place only if we are looking at the same thing at the same time with the same intensity. It also implies, doesn't it, that one has to listen not to mere words, their referents, and their dictionary meaning, not therefore giving your own particular meaning to the word, but rather listening to the word as well as the dictionary meaning. When you can listen like that, we share something. I feel we should do that in all these discussions.

I think the central problem of our existence is thought, the whole machinery of thinking, and I would like to go into that because our civilization both in the East and in the West is based on thought, on the intellect. Thought is very limited, measurable, though it has done the most extraordinary things— the whole area of technology, going to the moon, the possibility of building houses for everybody. But thought has also done a great deal of mischief—all the instruments of war, the destruction of nature, the pollution of the earth, and also, if one goes into it very deeply, thought has created the so-called religions throughout the world. Thought has been responsible for the mythology of the Christians with their savior, popes, priests, salvation, and all the rest of it. And thought has also been responsible for a particular kind of culture with its technological and artistic development, together with cruelty, brutality in relationship, class division, and so on. Thought is mechanical, leads to a mechanistic philosophy, mechanistic physics, and thought has divided human beings as the "me" and the "not me," the "we" and "they," the Hindu, the Buddhist, the Communist, the Socialist, the young and the old, the hippies, the bourgeois, the established order, and so on. All that structure is the result of thought. I think that is fairly clear, in the religious, secular, and political, including national, spheres.

As I have said, thought has created an extraordinary world— the marvelous cities, which are decaying, rapid transportation, and all that. But thought has also divided human beings in their relationships. Thought, which is the response of memory, experience, knowledge, divides human beings. That is, thought has built in our relationships with each other, through a series of incidents, activities, the image of the "me" and the "you": the images that exist through constantly interacting relationship. These images are mechanistic, and therefore relationship itself becomes mechanical.

There is not only the division brought about by thought in the outside world, but also the division inwardly in the human being. And one sees thought is absolutely necessary; otherwise you can't go to your house, you can't write a book, you can't talk—you can do nothing without thinking. But thinking is the response of memory, knowledge, and experience, which is the past. Thought projects the future through the present, modifying it, shaping it, designing it as the future.

If thought is impersonal, based on the accumulated knowledge of science and the accumulation of ideas, it has a logical and efficient function. Knowledge is important, but knowledge—that which is known—prevents the mind from going beyond the present and the past. Thought can function only in the field of the known, though it may project the unknown according to its conditioning, to its knowledge of the known. And you observe this phenomenon throughout the world—the ideal, the future, the *what should be*, what is bound to happen according to the background, to conditioning, education, the environment. And thought is responsible also for behavior, the vulgarity, crudeness, brutality, violence in relationships, and so on.

Now, thought is measurable, and I do not know if you have noticed, or reflected on it, that the West is the explosion of Greece, which thought in terms of measure. For the Greeks, mathematics, logic, philosophy—all the things they discovered, which exploded in the West—are the result of measurement, which is thought. Does this interest you? Because without an understanding of the whole machinery of thought, its tremendous significance, and where it becomes utterly destructive, meditation has no meaning. So unless you really understand, have a deep insight into the whole machinery of thinking, you cannot possibly go beyond it.

And in the East, India exploded over the whole of Asia, not among today's Indians but among the ancient Indians. Today's

Indians are just like Westerners: romantic, vulgar, superstitious, frightened, grabbing money, wanting position, power, prestige; all that business that goes on all over the world, only they are a different color, have a different climate, a partially different morality. But the ancient Indians said measurement is illusion, because when you can measure something it is very limited, and if you base all your structure, morality, and existence on measurement, which is thought, then you can never be free. Therefore they said, at least according to what I have observed, that the immeasurable is the real and the measurable is the unreal, which they call *maya*.

But thought—as the intellect, the capacity to understand, to observe, to be able to think logically together, design, construct—thought shaped the human mind, human behavior, in India too, as it does throughout Asia. In Asia they said that to find the immeasurable you must control thought; you must shape it through righteous conduct, through control of behavior, through various forms of personal sacrifice, and so on. It is exactly the same thing as in the West. In the West too they said control, behave, don't hurt, don't kill, but both the East and West nonetheless misbehaved, killed, did everything.

So thought is the central issue of our existence, which we cannot possibly deny. We can imagine that we have a soul, that there is a God, that there is a heaven, a hell, invent all these things by thought, both the nobility and the ugliness of existence, but all these are the product of the machinery of thinking. So if the world, outer existence, is the result of mechanistic philosophy, mechanistic physics, what place has thought in relationship, and what place has thought in the investigation of the immeasurable? If there is the immeasurable. Are you following all this? You must find out, and this is where we are going to share together.

I want to find out what significance thought, and therefore thinking, has in our existence. And if thought is measurable and therefore very limited, can thought investigate something that is not of time, of experience, of knowledge? You understand my question? Both the East and the West have asked whether the immeasurable—call it the unknown, the unnameable, the eternal, the everlasting, there are dozens of names for it—can be investigated by thought. For if thought cannot investigate it, then what is the mind that is capable of entering into that dimension that is wordless? Because the word is thought. We use a word to convey a particular idea, a particular thought, a particular feeling. So thought, which is concerned with remembering, imagining, contriving, designing, calculating, and therefore functioning from a center that is the knowledge accumulated as the "me"—can that thought investigate something that it cannot possibly understand? Because it can only function in the field of the known, otherwise thought is puzzled, is incapable of really operating. Is this clear?

So what is thinking? I want both of us to be very clear, to find out what thinking is, and to discover its right place. We said thinking is the response of experience, knowledge, of memory stored in the brain cells. Therefore, thought is the result of development, evolution, which is time. So thought is the result of time. Thought can function only within the space it creates around itself. And that space is very limited, that space is the "me" and the "you." Thought, the whole machinery of thinking, has a rightful place, and thought in relationship between two human beings becomes destructive. Do you see this?

Thought is the product of knowledge, time, evolution, the result of mechanistic philosophy and science, which are in their turn all based on thought, though occasionally a new discovery takes place in which thought doesn't enter at all. That is, you discover something totally new, and that discovery is not the discovery of thought. You *translate* what you have discovered in terms of thought, in terms of the known. A great scientist—I am not

talking of the political scientist who panders to governments—
may have immense knowledge, but that knowledge is absent at
the moment of seeing something new. Having an insight into
something totally new, he then translates it into the known, into
a word, into a phrase, into logical sequences. And such thinking
is necessary.

And such knowledge is absolutely essential. You can add to
it, take away from it, it can be increased, decreased, but the immensity of knowledge is a human necessity. Now, is knowledge
necessary in a relationship between human beings? Have you understood my question? We are related to each other, we are
human beings, we live on the same earth, and it is our earth, not
the Christian, the English, or the Indian earth; it is our earth,
with its beauty, its marvelous riches, it is our earth to be lived
on. And what place has thought in relationship? Relationship
means to be related, relationship means to respond to each other
in freedom, with responsibility. So what place has thought in relationship? Thought, which is capable of remembering, imagining, contriving, designing, calculating, and all that—what place
has it in human relationship? Has it any place, or no place at all?
Please, we are inquiring into ourselves, not mechanically somewhere else.

Is thought love? Don't deny it, we are inquiring, we are going
into it. What is our relationship when we live together in a house,
as husband, wife, friend, or whoever it is? What is our relationship? Is it based on thought? Which is also feeling, the two cannot be divided. If it is based on thought, then relationship
becomes mechanistic. And for most of us the relationship we
have with each other is mechanistic. By mechanistic I mean the
image created by thought about you and about me. The images
that each one creates, defends, over a number of years or over a
number of days. You have built an image about me and I have
built an image about you, which is the product of thought. The

image becomes the defense, the resistance, the calculation, building a wall around myself, and as I build a wall around you, you build a wall around yourself and you build a wall around me. This is called relationship, and it is a fact.

So our relationship is the product of thought, calculated, remembered, imagined, contrived. And is that relationship? It is easy to say, "No, of course not." When you put it so clearly, of course it isn't. But the fact is, it *is* our relationship, if we don't deceive ourselves. I don't want to be hurt, I don't mind hurting you, and so I build a resistance and you do the same. This process of interrelationship becomes mechanistic and destructive. And it being mechanistic, destructive, we try consciously or unconsciously to escape.

So I discover, I have an insight that any kind of interference of thought in relationship becomes mechanistic. I have discovered it. To me that is an immense fact—just as I see that a snake or a precipice is dangerous and destructive, I see that when thought interferes in relationship it is destructive. So what am I to do? I see thought is necessary at a certain level, and thought in relationship is most destructive. That is, you have hurt me, said things to me, flattered me, given me pleasure, sexual or otherwise, all the rest of it, nagged me, bullied me, dominated me, brought about frustration—those are all the images, the conclusions I have about you. And when I see you, I project all that. I may try to control it, I may try to suppress it, but it is always there.

So what is one to do? You understand my question? I see, I have an insight into the whole machinery of thinking, the whole machinery, not just in one direction but the machinery of thinking in human existence. Outwardly and inwardly, it is the same movement. And if the mind is to go beyond and above it, how is thought to be given enough scope to play with, without bringing about its own frustration? Come on, do you see the beauty of all this?

Life without understanding, without coming to, that state of something that can never be entered into by thought becomes very mechanical, routine, boring, tedious, you know all this. And knowing that it is boring, lonesome, dreadful, ugly, with occasional pleasure or joy, we want to escape, to run away from this horror. And therefore we imagine, we create myths, and myths have a certain place. The Christian myth has held people together. The Indians have great myths, and these myths have brought about a unity, and when the myths fade, fragmentation takes place, which is what is happening in the world at the present time. But if you really think about this very seriously, you have no myths about Christ, Jesus, or Buddha. You have dropped all that.

So how is the mind to bring about a harmony in which there is no division between the known and freedom from the known? The known as knowledge, the functioning of thought, and freedom from it. The two moving together, the two in perfect harmony, in balance, in the beauty of movement. Have you understood the question and the beauty of that question? Not an integration of the two, which is impossible, because integration means putting parts together, adding new parts, or taking away old parts. That implies an entity that is capable of doing this, an outsider, which is the invention of thought. Like the soul, or the *atman* in India, and so on, it is still thought. So my question is, Can they be like two rivers joining together, moving together, the known and the unknown, freedom from the known and a mind that has insight into a dimension in which thought doesn't happen at all? Have you got it?

Is this possible? Or is it merely an idea, merely a theory? The word *theory* means to have an insight, to have the capacity to observe instantly the truth of something, to behold. Now, that is the problem. Thought and nonthought. Thought when I have to build a bridge, write a book, make a speech, calculate where I shall go. And in relationship no thought at all, because that is love. Now, can the two move together all the time?

So thought says—listen to this carefully—I am asking the question, Can the two live harmoniously together? So that behavior is not based on thought, because then it becomes mechanistic, it conditions, it becomes a relationship of images. So can this movement of knowledge—because it is always moving, it isn't static, you are always adding—this movement in which there is thought as image-maker not come into relationship at all? If the question is clear, then you will see that thought, which is still operating, says, "To do that you must control. You must control thought, hold it, and not let it interfere in relationship, you must build a wall." So thought is calculating, imagining, remembering—remembering that somebody has said that these two movements must go together. So thought says, "I will remember that, it is a marvelous idea," so it stores it up as memory, and according to that memory it is going to act. Therefore it says, "I must control." And all mechanistic philosophy, civilization, all religious structure is based on control—the idea that after you have controlled, sufficiently suppressed, then you will be free, which is sheer nonsense! Are you working as hard as I am working? I don't know if you see the beauty of this!

So thought begins to create a pattern of how to behave in order to have that harmony. Therefore it has destroyed it! Now I have an insight. I have an insight into this question, that control is not the way. Control implies suppression, an entity who controls, which is still thought as the controller, the observer, the seer, the experiencer, the thinker. I have an insight into that. So what does the mind do?

How do you have an insight? What is insight? How does it take place? You know what I mean by insight: when you see something instantly as false and something as true. You do, on occasion. You see something totally and say, "By Jove, how true

that is." Now, what is the state of mind that says, "It is so,"—
which has nothing to do with thought, with logic, or dialectic,
which means opinion? What is the state of the mind that sees
the fact instantly, and therefore the truth of it? Obviously if the
thinker is there, there is no perception—the thinker, who is the
creator of will, which is the product of desire, because I want to
achieve that state, which must be extraordinary. So thought then
says, "I will bring about that state by suppression, control, by
various forms of sacrifice, asceticism, no sex, or whatever." It
goes through all that, hoping to come upon the other. The
other is accepted, because this is limited, this is tiresome, boring, mechanical, so in its desire to have more pleasure, more excitement, it will accept the other. The other is perhaps seen by
very few, or seen as an idea by a few, and because of that experience they say, "I am enlightened, I have got it"—and become
beastly little gurus.

So: we are now inquiring into what it is to observe without the
observer. Are we meeting? Because the observer is the past, the
known, is within the field of thought, the result of knowledge,
therefore experience and so on. So is there an observation without the observer, which is the past? Can I look at you, my wife,
my friend, my neighbor, without the image that I have brought
about through relationship? Can I look at you without all that
coming into being? Is that possible? You have hurt me, you have
said unpleasant things about me, you have spread scandalous rumors about me—I'm afraid you do, but it doesn't matter, pleas-
ant or unpleasant rumors are the same. And can I look at you
without bearing all that memory? Which means, Can I look at
you without any interference of thought, which has remembered
the insult, the hurt, or the flattery?

Can I look at a tree without the knowledge of that tree? Can
I listen to the sound of that river going by without naming, rec-
ognizing, saying that sound is made by the river—just listen to

the beauty of the sound? Can you do this? You may listen to the river, you may see the mountain without any calculated design, but can you look at *yourself* with all your conscious or unconscious accumulations, look at yourself with eyes that have never been touched by the past? Have you tried any of this? Sorry, I shouldn't have said "tried." To try is wrong. Have you *done* it? Looked at your wife, your girlfriend, boyfriend, or whatever it is, without a single memory of the past? Then you discover that thought is repetitive, mechanical, and relationship is not; therefore you discover love is not the product of thought. So there is no such thing as divine love and human love. There is only love. Do you follow all this?

Our life is based on thought, the whole machinery of thinking, the whole machinery of words, which we use, for example, to communicate through a novel. And without the word is there thought? Or is the mind such a slave to words that it cannot see the movement of thought without the word? That is, can I, can the mind, observe me, the whole content of me, without the word? Observe what I am without association—the association being the word, memory, remembrance—so that there is a learning about myself with no remembrance, without the accumulated knowledge as experience of anger, jealousy, antagonism, or desire for power. So can I look at myself—not "I"—can the mind look at itself without the movement of the word? Because the word is the thinker, the word is the observer.

Now, to look at yourself so clearly the mind must be astonishingly free from any attachment, whether to a conclusion, which is an image, or to any principle or idea that is the product of thought and put together by words, phrases, and concepts, and be free from any movement of fear and pleasure. Such perception is in itself the highest form of discipline—discipline in the sense of learning, not conforming. Are you capable of following all this?

We began with inquiring into and sharing the question, What is the place of thought in existence? For at present the whole of our life is based on thought. Thought may imagine it is not, that it is based on something spiritual, but that is still the product of thought. Our gods, our saviors, our masters, our gurus are the product of thought. So what place has thought in life, in existence? It has its place logically, sanely, effectively when knowledge functions, is used, without the interference of the "me," the "me" who says, "I am a better scientist than that person" or "I am a better guru than that guru." So knowledge, when used without the "me" that is the product of thought, which creates the division between you and me, is then the most extraordinary thing, because that will bring about a better world, a better structure of the world, a better society. We have enough knowledge to bring about a happy world, where we can all have food, clothing, shelter, no ghettos, but that is denied because thought has separated itself as the "me" and the "you," my country and your country, my beastly god and your beastly god, and we are at war with each other.

So thought has, as memory, remembrance, imagination, design, a logical and healthy place, but it can never come into relationship. If you see that—not logically, not verbally, not with the sense "I will be happier if I do that," not through words, through imagination, through formulas—if you see the truth of it, you are there. Then there is no conflict, and it happens as naturally as fruit ripening on a tree.

Are there any questions?

QUESTIONER: I feel that I am real.

KRISHNAMURTI: The gentleman says that he feels he is real. I wonder what we mean by saying, "I am real." I am sitting here, I have got a body, I see things about me, my thoughts are real, the words I use are real, I like and I don't like—that is real. You have hurt me, you have flattered me—that is real. My gods, I realize, I have invented. It is me out of fear that has produced these things. It is my pleasure that makes me attached to you, and therefore out of that pleasure I say, "I love you." In a certain way these are all real. Words are real. But if you are caught in words, they create illusion. So there is a certain reality that is obvious, and illusion begins when thought produces, out of fear and pleasure, the image of reality.

Q: What is the relationship between the body and thought?

K: If I had no body, would I be able to think? The whole organism with its nerves, its sensitivity, all the operative mechanical processes of the physical system, without that would there be thinking? If I had no brain, with its cells, which hold memory, which is connected with the whole body through nerves, would there be thinking?

Now, listen to this carefully. When the body dies—you see, now we all pay attention!—when the body dies, what happens to the thought that we have created—you understand? Are you following all this, does it interest you? I have lived thirty, fifty, one hundred years, I have spent most of my time working in an office, God knows why, earning a livelihood, fighting, quarreling, bickering, jealous, anxious, you know, my life, the dreadful thing that I live. And I die, the body dies, which is inevitable, through old age, disease, accident, pain, and I remember all that. All that is me. Is that "me" different from the body? Go into it very carefully. Is that "me" different from the instrument? Obviously it is different. The "me" is the result of my remembering the hurts, the pain, the pleasures, all that remembrance, which is stored up in the cells as thought, right? Will that thought go on when the body dies? Are you following all this? You have asked that question, sir—my brother and my friend whom I have remembered, loved, walked with, enjoying things together, that friend, brother, or my son, or husband dies. And I remember him and wonder, Does he exist? You are following all this? I am attached to him and I don't want to lose him. I have lost him physically. But I don't want to lose him. See what takes place. I don't want to lose him, I have a great memory, experience, pleasure, pain about him or her. I am attached to that, and I hold on to that.

So thought says, "He does live, we will meet next life, or we will meet in heaven. I like that idea, it gives me comfort," and you come along and say, "What nonsense, you are just a superstitious old man," and I fight you, because this idea gives me great comfort. So what I am seeking is comfort, not the truth of anything, but comfort. Now, if I do not seek comfort in any form, what is the fact? If I have lived a shoddy, narrow, petty, jealous, anxious life, like millions of people do, what is the importance of me? I am like the vast ocean of people. I die. You follow? But I cling to my little life, I want it to continue, hoping that at some future date I will be happy. And with that idea I die. And I am like a million others in a vast ocean of existence, without meaning, without significance, without beauty, without any real thing. And if the mind steps out of that vast stream, as it must, then there is a totally different dimension. And that is the whole process of living: to move away from this vast current of ugliness and brutality. And because we can't do it—we haven't got the energy, the vitality, the intensity, the love of it—we move along with it.

Q: Why do you speak of a blissful state? It holds out a promise of something other than what is for us. If thought is not there, consciousness can never know about it, so why talk about it? It is your talk of a blissful state that keeps us all coming.

K: Do you all come because I talk about a blissful state? Oh my God, I hope not! Look, sir, what is important is not the blissful state of somebody else. What is important is to understand *what is*. *What is* means *your* state, not my blissful state or X's blissful state. And to understand it, you must have tremendous energy, and that is what we are concerned with here, not to achieve somebody else's blissful state, which is then an illusion. You ought to kick that overboard! What we are concerned with is the understanding of *what is* and going beyond it. The understanding of thought, which is *what is*, the structure and nature of thought, which is *what is*, and seeing its right place and its destructive nature. And to see the freedom from the known and the known moving together, whether you can find that out, because it is your life, your existence not mine, not Mr. Nixon's or Mr. Heath's or Mr. somebody else's or the Communists' or the Pope's, or even that of Jesus—it is your life. And if you yourself know actually *what is*, then you will be beyond it.

There are so many questions, what am I to do?

Q: I who am neurotic wonder if being with a person who seems to be sane can help me to become sane too?

K: If you know you are neurotic, you have already stopped being neurotic. But most of us are not aware that we are neurotic, and being unaware that we are neurotic, we hope to become nonneurotic by being with somebody else. But this somebody else, who you who are neurotic think is sane, is also neurotic. This is not just a clever statement. If I am neurotic and I think you are sane, how can I know that you are sane if I am neurotic? [*laughter*] No, please. How do I know that you are enlightened—please listen to this—that you are the savior, that you have achieved heaven, when I am in misery? How do I know? I can't. But I would like to think you are in heaven because that gives me comfort. On that all our religions are based, which is so utterly silly. So if I am aware that I am neurotic that is enough.

Now, at what depth are you aware that you are neurotic? Who told you that you are neurotic? Have you found that out for yourself? Or have your friends kindly told you that you are neurotic? [*laughter*] Have you found out for yourself that you are neurotic, that you do not act sanely? Or have you watched people who you think act sanely and have compared yourself with them and therefore say, "I am neurotic"? When you compare you are neurotic. When you who are neurotic assert that somebody else is sane, that person is not sane.

So what is important is to be *aware*, deeply, profoundly, that you are not balanced. That very awareness dispels neuroticism. If I am aware that I am angry, jealous, or seek power, position, prestige, all of which are forms of neuroticism, if I am aware of that, I want to find out if I am aware only verbally, intellectually, just as a conclusion, an idea, or have I gone beyond it, deeper? Then if words, conclusions, ideas are pushed aside then I am really aware what I am. In that awareness am I insane, am I neurotic? Obviously I am not. It is these things that make me neurotic. Have you got it?

# 4 ᦉ WIPING OUT PSYCHOLOGICAL HURT

WE HAVE DISCUSSED previously the nature of thought, memory, knowledge, and experience and the deeply destructive place thought has in daily relationship. At the same time, knowledge as thought and expression in action is absolutely necessary. I do not know how deeply you have gone into this, but it seems to me that if we are at all serious, we have to explore this deeply. Not only because the times demand that we be very, very earnest, but also we lead rather superficial lives in the sense of giving full vent, full expression to the whole field of thought in everyday living, which I call superficial. So if you have gone into it, what place has thought in the whole of consciousness? And how deeply are the unconscious, hidden parts, the secret recesses of our mind, contaminated by the environment, by the society in which we live, through education, and so on? How deeply is the whole mind polluted, and is it possible to free the mind altogether from the pollution of this "civilization"? Can the mind ever be really free in the true sense of that word?

That can be seen only when we understand, have an insight into, the whole question of thought. So what I would like to do now is to go into this issue of how deeply thought has conditioned the mind, how deeply the culture in which we live has shaped the whole consistency of thought, for thought is a material process.

I would like to point out again that we are not merely indulging in theories, speculations, or concepts, but rather sharing, exploring together the question of whether the mind, which has been deeply conditioned for millennia through every form of culture, society, environmental influence, can possibly be "cleansed"; whether we can see how deeply we are affected; whether it is possible to expose the deep contents of oneself so completely that the mind is really totally clear and therefore free.

You know, we shouldn't say anything verbally that we have not actually directly perceived, otherwise we become hypocrites, otherwise we use other people's ideas, conclusions, and their illusions. They become the authority and we merely follow. Whereas if you could put aside all the external authority of others and their knowledge, and investigate this question yourself, have direct perception yourself, then what you say will be true to you. And then one acts tremendously honestly. So I feel we could perhaps spend a little time together inquiring how deeply we are secondhand, how deeply we accept what others say, and repeat it so glibly and easily, cleverly, just reacting to what others say.

What we are going to find out together, if we can, is whether the mind, your mind, the mind of the human being, can be totally unconditioned, and therefore act in freedom and yet together with others. Society, by which the speaker means the culture, the various economic divisions, social activities, has created in us an image, right? Now, please don't accept anything that the speaker says. You have to be able to completely deny everything everybody, especially the speaker, says psychologically, so that you don't set him up as an authority, so that you see directly for yourself and what you see will be yours.

As we have said, the culture in which we live, culture being the economic conditions, the religious divisions, the class struggles, the various forms of conformity and of imitation, has created in each of us an image of ourselves. That is, you have an image about yourself, haven't you? Not just one, perhaps half a dozen. How do these images come into being? Who has created these images? Surely it is culture and all its influences—religious, psychological, educational, environmental, economic—that has created in the human mind the image of what I am, or what I should be. I think there is no question about this. If I am born in a particular environmental state, I accept that from childhood—I am for the rest of my life a Catholic, a Protestant, a Hindu, a Communist, or whatever it is, a nationalist. And that image is deep-seated, it is the formula by which I live. The "me" *is* that formula. Please observe this. Not my description of it but the actual fact of it. The description is not the described. I can describe a mountain, but the description is not the mountain.

So this image is the whole of our consciousness. The content of consciousness *is* consciousness. Are we sharing this together? It is a lovely morning, really we should be out, looking at the deep shadows, the lovely mountains, the flowing waters, and the still, damp woods, which have a scent, a beauty of their own. But here we are, trying to be awfully serious, and we should be terribly serious, because we have to create a totally different kind of civilization, a totally different kind of human being. Not a freak, a Jesus freak, a Krishna freak, or a Marxist freak, but a totally different kind of human being who has understood himself completely and gone beyond himself.

So we have an image of ourselves. That image is part of our thought. Superficially, outwardly, that image shows very little, but inwardly it is deep-seated. Can that deep conditioning, those deep roots of the image, be exposed, understood, and gone beyond? That is the question I would like to discuss. Outwardly I show myself very little; like an iceberg, one-tenth is above and nine-tenths are below. What is below, hidden, secret, unexplored, never seen consciously—can that be completely exposed, so that there is no contradiction between the outer and the inner; so that there is a total awareness, a total insight; so that the mind, which is so fragmented, so broken up, can be free, whole, and sane? That is my question. I do not know if you have ever put it to yourself, and if not, we are putting it now, and you have to face it. How you regard it, how you face it, depends on your intensity, your interest, your energy and vitality.

This image, this conclusion, has various symbols, various names, but that is irrelevant. We'll keep to the word *image*—the two words *image* and *conclusion*. This image is constantly receiving both outer and inner impressions. Every word that is said in friendship or enmity has its effect. That image gets hurt from childhood. We human beings hurt each other terribly. That image, which society and thought have created, gets not only hurt but also flattered. So there is this constant process of being hurt, resisting, building a wall around myself. The superficial hurts can perhaps be dealt with, which is comparatively easy, but we are asking this: Can the deep hurts of the human mind be wiped away so that no mark of hurt is left?

You are hurt, aren't you, from childhood, when your mother, your father, your teacher, your aunt, somebody, says, "You are not as good as your brother," "You are not as clever," "You don't look so nice," "You look like your ugly aunt." Don't you know all these things? And then at school you are compared with another boy for marks or standards, and the comparison hurts very deeply. When you compare one boy with another one, you are destroying that boy. So all that hurt remains, which in later life expresses itself in violence, in anxiety, and so on as escapes from the hurt. And it escapes into illusion, which is another form of image, the illusion that you will never be hurt again, which is a state of neuroticism. Right? Please look at yourself. The words that the speaker is using are a mirror in which you are looking at yourself.

Now, the question is whether those hurts can be wiped out completely, so that there is not a single mark of hurt left, and so that a mind that has been hurt and has understood can never be hurt again. Because, after all, innocence is a state of mind in which there is no hurt. The word *innocent* means not to be hurt and not to hurt. Not the Christian meaning of the lamb and all that, but a mind that is not capable of being hurt and therefore doesn't hurt. We will go into that.

How is this possible? I have been hurt all my life, I am sensitive. You know what hurt is, the wounds that one receives, and what effect it has in later life. I have been hurt. I find I can deal with superficial hurts fairly intelligently. I know what to do. I can resist, build a wall around myself, isolate myself so that I will never be hurt, grow a thick skin—which is what most people do. But behind that they are deeply wounded. Or one can deal with hurt not building any resistance, but be superficially vulnerable. Because it is only a mind that is vulnerable that can never be hurt. Are you following this? Have you ever noticed a spring leaf? A new leaf just coming out after a heavy winter in the bright warm sunlight, and that leaf is so tender, so alive, and the breezes, the winds, can never tear it, it is there. That is vulnerability.

So one can intelligently bring this about outwardly, superficially. But the question is, How deeply can all the hurts be wiped away? That is, how can the unconscious hurts, these deep hurts, how can they be wiped away? Can it be done through analysis? Please watch this carefully. If you see the truth of it once, you will never do anything but the right thing. Can these hurts be wiped away through analysis? The root meaning of the word *analysis* is to break up. You break up whatever it is in analysis. But who is the entity that is analyzing the broken parts? It is another part of thought, isn't it? Thought itself is a fragment of the total. You are following all this? So one thought examines, analyzes the various fragments of other thoughts, which is to continue fragmentation. If you see that, if you have an insight into that, you will never analyze. Have you got an insight into that?

Analysis means the analyzer, time, and each analysis must be complete. Otherwise there is a remnant, and the next day that remnant examines. Therefore you are always dealing with remnants, not with a complete end of analysis. And if you analyze, it takes days, months, years. So if you see the truth of that, the danger of it, then you will never indulge privately or publicly in any form of analysis. Can I go on from there? That means you have stopped analyzing, whether collectively, personally, or through a professional.

So analysis is not going to expose the secret, deep hurts. Then what will you do? After hurts, I'll take other things, so please follow this carefully. What will you do? I will not analyze, I see the foolishness of it—not because the speaker says so; you yourself see it. Therefore what shall I do? How to expose the secret, deep hurts? Will dreams expose them? And are dreams necessary? The professional analysts and psychologists say that you must dream, otherwise you will go mad. Dreams are the continuation of what we do during the day. Obviously. If we are conscious of what we are doing during the day, of our thoughts, our feelings, our reactions, playing with them, and watching them, not taking them terribly seriously, but watching them, then are dreams necessary when we go to sleep?

So if analysis and dreams are not the way, then what is? How does the mind wipe away all the hurts, the hurts that one has received from friends, from casual acquaintances, from intimate relationship—how is this done? Are you waiting for an answer from me? Are you? I am afraid you are. Now, just a minute, if there was nobody to answer it, nobody, what would you do? You have discovered for yourself that analysis is not the way. You have discovered for yourself that dreams have their value at a certain period of life but have intrinsically no value. If during the day you are alive, watching, listening, taking everything into account, going beyond the words, then dreams have very little value, because you are awake, you are alive, full of energy, without any contradiction, or watching every kind of contradiction. Then as you go to sleep, you will find dreams are not necessary, and therefore the mind, the brain, has complete rest. It is this conflict during the day that destroys the mind, the brain.

If you put order in your life during the day, the brain hasn't got to put order during the night. Have you understood? Come on, move! And order can be brought about only when you understand the disorder in which you live. Understanding disorder, not what is order. If you create order then it will be a blueprint, won't it? Whereas if one begins to understand the nature of disorder in one's life—the ugliness, the pettiness, the quarrels, the nagging, the gossip, the stupidities that go on, everlastingly giving and offering opinions—then in understanding disorder, order naturally comes in.

Now, if there is nobody to answer you, to tell you, what is your answer when you are faced with this question, which is, How are the deep hurts to be wiped away so that the mind can never be hurt? You, who are very clever people, who have read a great deal and can quote Freud, Jung, and all the professionals, what is your answer? Please be honest, what is your answer? Can you honestly say, "I really don't know"? Now, please be careful, can you truthfully, with integrity, say, "I really don't know"? Or is your mind still searching to find an answer in books, or in people who have said there is an answer? Come on. Can you really truthfully, honestly say, "I really don't know. I have no answer. I know what the problem is, I am fully aware of its meaning, significance, and depth. I have looked at it, watched it, viewed it from different angles, worried about it, examined it, but I have no answer."?

What makes it a problem—please listen carefully—what makes it a problem? *A problem exists only when you want to resolve it.* Please listen to this carefully. I have a problem: I want to have a mind that is clear, unhurt, unpolluted, free, vital, full of beauty and energy. And I have examined, looked at it, and I see analysis, interpreting dreams, is not the way, nor is going off to someone and saying, "Please help me" or following some guru who tells me, "Forget all that, think about God." I see all that is of no value. So I am left with this, and it has become a problem. And I say, Why has it become a problem? If I can't do anything about it, it is not a problem. You are following all this? It is only when I think I can do something about it that it becomes a problem. I don't know if you understand this?

If I actually know that I am confronted with a gigantic mountain, and I can't do anything about it—it is there, with its great height, dignity, majesty, full stability, splendor—why should I make a problem of it? It is only when I want to climb it, go beyond it, that it becomes a problem. But when I see that I can't do anything about this, is it a problem? If it is not a problem, then it is resolved, isn't it? This is not a trick, please. It is a truth. A river is flowing by, full, strong, heavy with water. It is only when I want to cross to the other side, where I think there is more freedom, more beauty, more loveliness, peace, and so forth, that crossing the river becomes a problem. But I see I can't cross the river—I haven't got a boat, I can't swim, I don't know what to do. Therefore what happens to my mind? It is not content with remaining on this side, you understand. But it has no problem. I wonder if you are getting all this? So my hurt is not a problem. Therefore I am not hurt. Oh, it is so simple if you see this! It is so simple that we refuse to see it.

Now, leave that for the moment and look at another issue.

The image that we have about ourselves is created by society, by the culture in which we live. The culture says, Compare, measure yourself against another. Compare yourself with the hero, with the saint, with a clever man, a man who puts words on pages or sculpts; compare yourself from beginning to end. You are doing this, aren't you, measuring yourself? Such measurement is part of our culture, and so you say to yourself, "I am clever" or "I am dull." You are dull in comparison with somebody who is clever, more learned, more subtle, more intelligent, more something— when you have a measure, there must be the more or the less, right? That is part of our culture. Now I am asking myself, Why do I have this measure? It has been given to me. Or I have care- fully cultivated it myself—the bigger car, the bigger house, the bigger mind, the gradual process of attainment. The whole process of our existence is based on measurement—the rich, the poor, the man who is healthy, the man who is unhealthy, the man who is a saint or a sinner.

Now, can the mind live without measurement, which means comparison? Can you? Have you ever tried to never compare psychologically? You have to compare when you get some cloth, I am not talking about that. You have to compare if you are building a house; there it is necessary, but is it necessary psycho- logically, part of our inheritance like Jesus, like the Buddha? We are brought up from childhood to measure, which is part of our hurt. If I have no measurement, I am not hurt. Now what am I to do? I measure. You sit there and the speaker sits on a plat- form; there is a division, high and low. And you say, "By Jove, how does that man sitting there know so much? I know so lit- tle." There is this everlasting comparison.

When you compare, you become inferior or superior. And through the comparison you come to a conclusion, and that con- clusion brings about neurotic habits. I conclude something through comparison, and I hold on to that conclusion irrespective of facts, of what is real. Because I have compared, watched, learned, I hold on. Haven't you noticed this? And that is a neurotic state, isn't it? Now, why do I compare? Partly habit, partly heredity, partly it is profitable, and through comparison I feel I am alive because I am struggling, I am fighting to be like you, and that gives me vitality—though I also get depressed and all the rest of it.

So now I am asking myself, Is it possible to live a life in which there is no comparison at all, and yet not be satisfied? When I cease to compare is there satisfaction with *what is*? Or when I cease to compare am I then face to face with *what is*, and when I compare there is an escape from *what is*? And therefore a waste of energy, and I need energy, there must be energy, to face *what is*. So are you dissipating energy through comparison? And if you are, and have an insight into all this, which is your insight, not mine, then you have energy that is not wasted through comparison, measurement, feeling inferior, superior, depressed, and all the rest of it. Therefore you have energy to face what actually is, which is yourself. How do you know that you are dull or unintelligent? Because you are comparing with somebody else, and therefore you say, "I am unintelligent"? If you don't compare, are you dull? Or you don't know, so you begin to face things. Come on, move!

So we have a great many images, a collection of religious, economic, and social images, images based on relationship, and so on. These images are deep-down conclusions. And if I do not analyze or use dreams as a means of analysis, if I am awake during the day and watch, then the problem is nonexistent. I wonder if you see this? Thought has created the problem. Thought that says, "Yes, that is so, I compare, I have images, I have been hurt, I must go beyond them"—it is thought that is saying this, and it is thought that created these images. So thought is creating a problem about the images. You are following? And when you see the truth of that, then thought doesn't make it a problem. For God's sake, see how extraordinarily simple and subtle and beautiful it is. If you see that once, it is finished! Then you have energy to face actually *what is*.

So then you can say, "What am I?" If I am no longer comparing, no longer imitating, and comparison means imitation, conformity, and if there are no hurts, no conclusions and therefore no image, what am I? Now, I am all these things: the thought that says, "I must analyze, I must go beyond this, I am in conflict, I must . . ."— you follow? It is thought that created all these images, divisions, and it is thought that says, "I must go beyond all this to live a peaceful, heavenly, quiet life of enlightenment." Which is not enlightenment, it is just an *idea* of enlightenment.

So then what am I? Do you understand? Am I the word? Am I the description? Am I the thought, which is the response of accumulated memory, experience, knowledge, which are all words, symbols, ideas? Then the mind is completely empty, right? Can the mind face this complete not being? You have understood? It is the wanting to be that is the problem. I wonder if you are getting all this? If you can't, I must go on. Sorry. Take what you can; what you can't, let go.

Civilization says to me, Be something, a success, join this community, grow long hair, short hair, take drugs, don't take drugs, go to church, don't go to church, be free, think independently. Society, whether it is small or large, is forcing me to conform to a pattern. And the pattern is my image, I am that image. I am the image that is described by the professionals, by myself when I am alone, the agonies of that image, the jealousies, the fears, the pleasures. And I see that all this image making is what makes the mind so utterly superficial. Do you agree, or do you *see* that? Are you aware that your mind is superficial? Or are you agreeing with this *description* of the superficial mind?

So can the mind be without comparison, without conformity? I conform when I put on trousers, right? When I go to India, I put on something else. I have to conform at a certain level, keep to the left or the right of the road. But psychologically there is no conformity anymore, because this urge to conform is the product of the society in which I live, the image that I have built in myself with the help of others. And I see that this image can be hurt; it is the image that gets hurt, it is the image that in comparison feels great or small, inferior or superior. And when there is no measurement, is there an image? Then the mind is capable of living without a single image, and therefore incapable of ever being hurt. Do you see this?

Only then can I have relationship. And I may have that relationship with you, but you may be hurt, and have an image about me, and you refuse to move from that image. Then the battle begins. Or you have no image, but I have an image. And I refuse to give up my image, because I love my image, that's my neuroticism, that's my conclusion. And where then is the relationship between you and me? There isn't any. You say you must have relationship. The neurotic person says you must always have relationship with everybody. How can I? How can you with me, who has and is holding on to an image?

So the mind is capable of living without a single image and therefore without any conclusion. So it can never be hurt or be in a state of measurement. It is only such a mind that is innocent and therefore free. Do you want to ask any questions about this?

You know, the speaker said previously that the content of consciousness *is* consciousness. Have you understood that? My consciousness is made up of nationalism, with innumerable things from my education. It is the content that makes up consciousness. And therefore the content makes the borders of that consciousness, fixes the frontiers, draws the line, because it is the content, however wide, however narrow, that determines what consciousness is. But if there are no contents, which are measurement, ideas, then what is consciousness? Does this interest you? I only know consciousness as the "me" in conflict. If there is no problem, no conflict, what is consciousness? Is there then any border, any frontier? There is no demarcation made by the content. Then there is space, isn't there? Space without a center, therefore no circumference. You know, that is what love is—because love has no dimension. We'll go into that later; I mustn't go into it now.

QUESTIONER: Does not all effort to unify in this conditioned state result in further diversity?

KRISHNAMURTI: The questioner says that we are always trying to unify, to bring about unity in a mind that is conditioned. I am conditioned and you are conditioned and we want to bring about a unity between you and me. I am conditioned as a drug taker, by all my experiences, and you don't take drugs, but you are conditioned in a different way. You are a Catholic and I am a Hindu, and we are trying to establish unity. The other day one of the high dignitaries of the Anglican Church was being interviewed, and he was asked what he thought of all the various religions in the world. "Oh," he said, "they have some truth in them, they are all right." But the questioner said, "What do you mean by 'all right'? Do you mean they have truth?" "Oh, partly, probably, a great deal," and he began to expatiate, enlarge on that. Then he said, "Do you know what is remarkable? In our religion we have the only thing that matters, which is Jesus Christ, and nobody else has." You understand? A twentieth-century high dignitary— I'll leave it at that!

Now, can there be unity between two conditioned minds? Or will there inevitably be conflict between two conditionings? Conditioning implies division. Where there is division there must be conflict. If you are my wife, and I am your husband, or if I am the wife, and you my husband have your own ambition and greed, and I have my own, I am conditioned to your conditioning. So though we are married and have children together, and all the rest of the business, we two are separate, conditioned human beings. And how can there be unity between us? And because there isn't, there is everlasting battle between us.

There can be unity only when there is no division. It is so simple. I am divided because of my images, my conclusions, my opinions. When I have no conclusion, no image, there is no division. That is love, you understand?

Now we, being conditioned, spend our energy in strife, in battles, in wars, in all that is going on in the world. And that is a tremendous waste of energy. That waste of energy may be productive, because I may have a little talent to write a book, and I become well known, I sustain my vanity through the book. But when there is no division, because I see the fact, the truth, that division—which is conclusion, image, comparison, all the rest of it—must inevitably create conflict; if I have an insight into that, if I see the truth of it, then I have an immense amount of energy to act totally differently from the way I do now.

Q: You say free and together. Would you please go a little further into this idea of together?

K: I can't go into the *idea* of together. Then it remains an idea, and how can you go further into an idea, which means more ideas? You can only go into it if you have no ideas. I don't know if you follow this?

Now, I said earlier that we are sharing, talking over our problem together. That means you and I are both interested in the problem. We are both concerned about it, examining the problem together—not I examine and you don't, and then you share what I examine. That is not *together*. *Together* implies moving together, that is, thought with thought, feeling with feeling, intensity with intensity. Do you know what it means to be together? I doubt it. It means sharing, partaking, investigating, examining, thinking together, so that there is no division between the one who thinks and the one who doesn't. But if we are both of us at the same time, at the same level, with the same intensity looking at a problem, we are together. And this is possible only when you give your *life* to this—and this is our life.

Q: You speak of the authority of beliefs, but never, or hardly ever, in any great depth of all that is involved in the authority of money, slavery, oppression, fear, and violence.

K: By Jove, you can ask questions, can't you?

The questioner says you talk about authority, but you never, or hardly ever, go into the authority of money, the authority of domination, the authority of slavery, poverty, and so on.

Now, what is the central issue here? There is the authority of money, the authority of those with power, whether religious or nonreligious, the authority of social division, of injustice, and so on. What is the central issue involved in this? There is not only the psychological authority of the priest or of Karl Marx, and the outward authority of knowledge, science, physics; there is also inward authority, the authority that I assume because I know better than you, I see more clearly than you, I happen to sit on many platforms, and therefore I assume tremendous authority. And there is the authority of the landlord who any day can throw me out of the house in which I live. So there is this tremendous, complex authority.

Now, where shall I begin? Are you meeting me? Where shall I begin to tackle this enormous, complex authority that exists outside as well as inside? You have asked the question, I want to go into it. Where shall I begin? Out there? With the authority of money, the authority of property, the authority that the poor and the rich have? Where will you deal with it? You are very silent. My question is, Where shall I begin? I see there is the authority of money—let us keep to that because money implies all the other things. But as well as the authority of money, there is the authority of ideas, of beliefs. So there is the authority of money outwardly, and there is the authority of tremendous knowledge, of which I am part.

Now, I see the danger of authority, because it enslaves the mind. If I am born, as I was, very poor, poverty is a degradation; it destroys. So the power of money is tremendous, and so is the power of idea, right? Marx, Jesus, Buddha, whoever it is. So I say to myself, where shall I begin to understand the vast, complex problem of authority? Where shall I begin? Attack money? Throw bombs at people who have money, who have houses, set fire to them, kill people because my authority says, "Having money and houses is wrong"? So where shall I begin? There or here? "There" is created by what is "here," the mind that worships authority, because I want that authority, I want the authority of money, the authority of property.

So I have to tackle authority where I am. Where I am is nearest, therefore I can begin here, not out there, because I can't do anything about that. I think I can by electing the right president or right minister, but when I trust, put faith in any politician, I am done for, finished, destroyed. So I don't put faith in any politician, any priest, any idea, or any power. Therefore I say, "I must begin here." That is, I want to find out why my mind worships authority in me, as well as out there. Why do I accept and worship and demand authority? Why do you demand it? Don't you demand it? Be honest. You do. Is it the basic issue of great pleasure? To own property, doesn't it give you tremendous pleasure, though incurring all the complications of taxes? It gives you prestige, a position, doesn't it? Oh, come on. Have you noticed the power a man has who has plenty of ideas, who has written books and is well known? And don't you want to be like that bird?

So we all worship power, in different forms. And to bring about a totally different kind of society, a different kind of culture, each of us must understand and have an insight into this question of authority. And be free of authority, not just talk endlessly about it.

# 5 ✺ THE FAILURE OF EDUCATION, SCIENCE, POLITICS, AND RELIGION TO END HUMAN SORROW AND CONFLICT

---

I WOULD LIKE TO TALK ABOUT something else that seems to me rather important. For the last two or three discourses we have been exploring the whole structure and nature of thought, and both the beneficial and the destructive roles that it plays in one's life. I think we ought to go now into the question of suffering, not only physical pain, disease, accident, and the ailments of old age, but also the whole psychological meaning of suffering. This has been one of the great problems of human beings. And apparently it has not been possible to solve it. One has run away from it, given various explanations, and the explanations are never the real thing. It has been avoided and rationalized, but it still remains. And if we could spend some time together on this question it might perhaps be very beneficial.

The Christian world has accepted sorrow and worships it in the form of a person, and the Eastern world has various logical and illogical explanations. But humankind remains in sorrow, not only personal sorrow but also immense collective sorrow—the sorrow of wars, where thousands are being killed, children are being burned. Not only recently but also during the last world war millions were killed in Russia—you know all that business. There is this immense collective sorrow, it is like an enormous cloud. And also there is personal, individual, human sorrow, which is caused by a sense of frustration, not being able to resolve any of life's problems, living always in ignorance—not ignorance in the sense of a lack of book knowledge, but ignorance of oneself, of what is going on within. And when one considers all this objectively and unsentimentally, why is it that you and I, human beings throughout the world, have not been able to resolve this question? Because without going beyond sorrow there is no love. Sorrow creates a circle around itself, either through self-pity or a sense of frustration through comparison—I was happy and now I am not—or through the sorrow of losing somebody whom you think you love.

Faced with this whole question of enormous human sorrow—whether collective, the result of appalling human behavior toward other human beings, what wars have done, what not only past but recent tyrannies have done, or your own particular sorrow—one observes how human beings, you, escape from this, avoid it, never come directly into contact with it. And without understanding, going into it, resolving it, without the *ending* of sorrow, however much one may seek, demand, or inquire into the nature of love, it seems to me impossible to find out what love is. Let us go into it.

What is sorrow? You have suffered both physically and psychologically. You have suffered when you have seen children starving, their poverty, what human beings have done to animals, to the earth, the air, how they kill each other at the least provocation for their country, for their God, for their king or queen, for their religion. And one has suffered oneself: Someone whom you love, or think you love, has gone, and there is this sense of immense loneliness, isolation, lack of companionship, the utter sense of forlornness. I am sure most of us have felt this in a crisis or vaguely in moments of unawareness. Unless one totally understands it, goes beyond it, there can never be wisdom. Wisdom comes with self-knowledge, or with the ending of sorrow. And you cannot buy wisdom in books or from another. It comes only when there is self-knowing and therefore the ending of sorrow.

Now, why does one suffer? We know when we have physical pain that we can do something about it or put up with it intelligently without becoming neurotic. That is, if I have constant physical pain, that pain can be understood and lived with, without distorting the mind, without bringing about action that is not only neurotic but also contradictory, aggressive, expressing itself in violence, and so on. Physical pain we can bear, tolerate, understand, and do something about logically and sanely, and perhaps also illogically and insanely. But we are discussing together—it is not my problem, please, it is your problem—what is sorrow, *why* does one suffer? And will the discovery of the cause of suffering end suffering? One may suffer because one is desperately lonely. In such loneliness you have no sense of relationship with another, it is total isolation, and you feel this perhaps when you are alone in your room in the middle of the night. When you are in a crowd, sitting in a bus, or at a party, you feel suddenly utterly, hopelessly deserted by everything and there you are, utterly empty, utterly isolated. Haven't you felt all these things? Such loneliness is very painful, and we escape from it in various ways, through churchgoing, social work, marriage, children, companionship, or drugs—anything to escape from this great sense of isolation.

Now, how do you resolve this? We will go into it step by step. We are doing this together, please. It is not that I want to speak about it, therefore I am pushing it onto you, but it is the problem that all human beings have, whether rich or poor, whether tyrants or the most enslaved people. How does one go beyond this sense of utter loneliness, which is one of the factors of great sorrow? I don't know if you have even looked at this problem. Our gods, our churches, our literature, our ceremonies, you know, all the circus that goes on around us, including the Olympics—I saw an advertisement this morning, as I was coming along—exist to give us comfort. That has been the function of the priest: to help us tolerate this ugly life while promising a new life in heaven. So that becomes a marvelous escape from this sense of utterly despairing, lonely existence. And although we may be married, have children, and all the rest of it, there is still this isolation, which has been carefully built up through our daily activities: a self-centered existence culminating in this isolation. Now, what is one to do? How is one to resolve this problem?

First of all, just look at the problem clearly. I am lonely because in my daily life I have been ambitious, greedy, envious, making myself terribly important, isolating myself, though I may be married and all the rest of it. And this self-centered activity ultimately brings about this isolation, this sense of utter, empty loneliness. If you have not felt it, you are not a human being. Because you have escaped from it and so you are blind! And so we escape in various forms from one of the central issues of our life. Religion offers, you know, all the escapes that we have very carefully established through thought; it is thought that has produced our religions, our systems of meditation, our social work; and the despairing, destructive, appalling wars, killing animals and so forth, are the product of thought.

Now, what are you, a human being, to do when you are confronted with, aware of, this sense of loneliness, which is one of the factors of sorrow? During our daily existence we expend energy on being concerned with ourselves, and that energy is dissipated in activities that ultimately block all further expressions of energy, and that is loneliness. Are we together in this? Loneliness is after all a blocking of all energy. Before, I was aware that I was lonely and I expended energy on escapes of various kinds—trivial, nonsensical, brutal, so-called spiritual activities. Expending energy in this way has kept me going, but I suffer from loneliness and the energy gets completely blocked. I don't know if you realize this. It is quite interesting. And when energy is not expended through escapes then energy is concentrated. And when you don't escape there is passion. Passion. There are various forms of passion: sexual passion, passion to be great, trying to be better, trying to improve, trying to become some idiotic person.

So one realizes that whatever the form of escape, whether subtle, conscious, unconscious, deliberate, or act of will, it doesn't resolve this problem. On the contrary, it makes it worse, because in escaping you engage in all kinds of absurdly irrational activities. Whereas if you do not escape because you see the truth of that, have an insight into it, then this whole sense of loneliness disappears, and something else comes about, which is the sense of passion. You know, the root meaning of the word *passion* is sorrow. It is rather curious, isn't it? When there is sorrow and no escape whatsoever from it, none of the various subtle forms of escape, that sorrow becomes passion. And we are also inquiring why one suffers. Apart from loneliness, why does one suffer? Through self-pity? Do you know what self-pity is? And is it one of the reasons one suffers? Again, self-pity is concern with oneself: *You* have such a beautiful life and *I* have not. *You* are so brilliant, so famous, so et cetera, and *I* have nothing, my life is shoddy, petty, small. So through comparison and measurement, I feel inferior, and that is one of the causes of sorrow. Now, can the mind that is thought as measurement put an end to itself so that there is no self-pity whatsoever? Please, do this as we go along.

What are the other factors that bring sorrow in human life? I want to love. I love you, and you don't love me, and I want more love from you, I feel I must be loved by you. You are the only person who can love me, nobody else. I shut the door on everybody else except you. I will keep my door open to you. And you look the other way. Doesn't this happen to all of you? And you spend your life in sorrow, bitterness, anger, jealousy, frustration, because you insist on going through one door! And you find that you are not loved. I don't know if you have ever considered what a terrible thought it is that you are not loved. Isn't it appalling to feel that you are not loved?

Have you ever noticed a flower on the wayside, the beauty, the color of it? It has a perfume, and it isn't asking you to look at it, it isn't asking you to smell it—it is there. But we human beings have this mechanism of thought that says, "I must be loved, I haven't got enough love" or "I must love you." So one of the factors of our sorrow is the sense of not being loved, isn't it? And we demand that love be expressed in a certain way—sexually or in companionship, in friendship, platonically or physically. Which all indicates, doesn't it, a human mind demanding to have a relationship with another based on its own urgency, which prevents love coming into being. As we have said, there is love only when there is the ending of sorrow. Love cannot exist within the circle, the field, of sorrow.

Sorrow also exists where there is fear. So one has to explore why human beings are fearful. Why and what does a particular human being fear? What does fear mean basically? Isn't it a sense of insecurity? A child demands complete security. And increasingly, both the father and mother are working, and homes break up. When the parents are so deeply concerned with themselves, their social position, having more money, more refrigerators, more cars, more this and that, they have no time to give complete security to the child. Don't you know all this?

Security is one of the essential things of life, not only for you and me but for everybody. Whether you live in a ghetto or a palace, security is absolutely necessary. Otherwise the brain can't function efficiently and sanely. Watch this process, how it happens. I need security, I must have food, clothes, and shelter, and so must everybody. And if I am lucky I can cover these physical needs. But psychologically it becomes much more difficult to be completely secure. So I seek that security in a belief, a conclusion, nationality, a family, or in my experience, and when that experience, that family, my belief is threatened, there is fear. There is fear when I have to face danger, the psychological danger of uncertainty, meeting something I don't know, the tomorrow. And there is fear when I compare myself with you who I think is greater than me.

So can the mind have security? Can the brain have complete security in which every form of fear has come to an end? Please listen to this. I am afraid, because I see that the brain demands security that cannot be disturbed, so that it can function effectively, sanely, rationally. And when it cannot there is fear. I see that very clearly. Now, how is the brain to find complete security so that there is no fear? How is your mind and brain, which are the same thing, from which your thought, your whole being, begins—how is that brain to have total security so that at no time, either consciously or unconsciously, it is caught in fear, the fear of uncertainty, the fear of not knowing or being incapable of finding out? Now, how is this to take place? Will there be security in any belief, conclusion, opinion, or knowledge? Obviously not, though human beings have tried those things.

Can the mind realize that there is no security in the things that thought projects? Thought has projected belief, projected conclusions; thought has created dogmas, rituals, saviors, all these outer psychological conclusions upon which it relies. And when they are threatened, there is terrible fear. And most intelligent, awakened people have put all that aside, some of them perhaps completely. They no longer go to church, no longer accept any form of Marxist theory, and so on.

So how is the mind to be secure? Which is absolutely necessary, because insecurity is one of the major causes of fear. And
what is intelligence? Because if the mind is intelligent there is no
fear. If the mind is capable of meeting life intelligently—I am
going to find out what intelligence is presently—and is awake, it
can meet any situation fearlessly. And so the mind itself becomes
the sense of security. I don't know if you see this. The mind, as
it exists now, is confused. We don't know what to do, we don't
know what to think, we have put our faith in something, and that
has failed; we have believed in something, and that has failed. We
have relied on tradition, and that has gone. We have relied on
friends, relationships, family, and everything has broken down.
So the mind is utterly confused, uncertain, seeking, asking. Isn't
that true of most of us?

And so what shall a mind that is confused do? A confused
mind mustn't do a thing. Because whatever it does out of that
confusion will be confused. Whatever choice it makes must be
confused. It will be confused in following any leader. The leader
must be confused too, otherwise you wouldn't accept him. Do
you see this? If you are following somebody, your guru, the
guru must be confused, because you are confused, otherwise
you wouldn't follow him. Oh, do see all this! Give your heart to
this, be passionate about it, and you will find out. So what do
you do when you are confused? We generally ask somebody to
help us to be clear; we read some philosophy and escape
through that, or through something else, which are all actions
from confusion, and so are bound to lead to more confusion,
misery, and conflict.

So what am I to do when I know I am confused? I know there
must be complete security, and I am confused. Therefore I will
not do a thing! You understand? I am confused because I thought
I could *do* something to clear up this confusion. I thought I could
go beyond confusion, but the entity that says I am going beyond

the confusion is part of the confusion and is the creator of the confusion. Therefore thought, which has brought about confusion, says, "I can't do a thing about it." The moment that it realizes it cannot do anything about it, confusion ends. Come on! So the mind then becomes very clear.

As we have said, we have put our faith, our belief, in something, in education, science, politics, religion, and everything has failed. If you don't see that, you are not aware.

Now, where shall the mind find its own security? It finds its own security when it sees what is false, what is illusion, when it sees it has no insight. The moment it *has* an insight, that very insight *is* security, which is intelligence. Have you got it? I see, have an insight, am aware, see the truth that any kind of organized religion is destructive. That is the truth. And the very perception of that is security. I see very clearly, have an insight that if there is an image between you and me, that image prevents relationship. The insight into that is security. I see, there is a perception, that any form of escape from loneliness is destructive, has no value. That very perception *is* security. And that is intelligence. So there is complete security in this intelligence. Are you getting it? And so fear doesn't exist.

That is, one is afraid, not only of the dark, not only of physical pain, not only of what people say about you, but there is fear of death, of life, of almost everything. And there are not only conscious fears but also the hidden fears, the unconscious deep-rooted fears, which you suddenly discover. Now, how shall the mind deal with them? Because I see very clearly that any fear, whether physical or psychological, brings about a state of darkness, a state of misery, confusion, ugliness, and sorrow. I see it, not as an intellectual perception but an actual perception that fear in any form is the most destructive thing. And there is deep-rooted fear inherited through the culture, through my family, through religion, and so on.

So how shall I deal with this? Has fear many heads or only one, many expressions or only one expression, which seems to have different forms? Are you getting tired of all this? Shall the mind pursue analytically every fear, every form, every expression of fear? Or is there only one central fear? You have to find out, haven't you? Do the many facets of fear make up the whole of fear, or is there only fear, one root of it that expresses itself in a variety of different ways?

I can see that tracing one fear, one expression of fear, comes to a central issue. Take one of your fears and go into it very deliberately, watching it; see if you can watch it, if you can objectify it and remain with it and not escape from it. Look at it, go into it step by step and you find the root. Then take another fear: Are the roots different? Or is there only one root with different branches, like a tree? If I can understand that one root completely, then it is finished, whether the fear of death, of loneliness, of losing my job, fear of my not being able to give a talk the day after tomorrow, fear of falling ill. Are they the various movements of this central fear? For me, there is only one fear, the root of it, like an expanding tree. And if the mind can go into that deeply, into the very complex root system, then to examine particular fears has no value.

Now, can the mind—listen to this—look not at the various expressions of the root but the whole root system? It can observe that root system completely only when the mind is not concerned with solving a particular fear. I am afraid of what my wife is going to say, of losing my job, of not being able to fulfill myself in some blasted little work. And I examine each of these fears and I come to the root thing, which is the desire, the will to be, the will to assert. And this desire to be, this demand in that root system for existence, is the factor that brings the various other fears. So can my mind look at this fear, live with it, not try to change it? Because the moment I exert will or choice upon it, my mind is working from confusion, from a conclusion, trying to go beyond it, therefore conflict, and conflict feeds fear.

So is the mind, your mind, capable of looking at the root of fear, not only the expressions of it? That means looking at the whole tree of existence in which one of the factors is fear. Now, how do you look at something totally? Not only the particular fear but the root fear; not only your particular idiosyncratic fears, your fears of various kinds, but the totality of human fear. How do you look at it? What does it mean to look at something totally? Are we meeting each other? Or are you going to sleep?

We are asking, How can the mind—listen to this—which is fragmented into the "me" and the "not me," we and they, my house, your house, my God, your God, my system and your system, my guru and your guru, my politics and your tyranny, how can such a mind look at the whole thing, at the totality of any problem? Unless it can look at the totality of it, it cannot resolve it and go beyond it. So how does it look—not *how* in the sense of the means—when does the perception of the total take place? That can happen only when thought—which by its very nature is fragmentary, which by its very nature must create confusion, and which creates my fear of tomorrow—realizes that it *is* fragmentary, and that it cannot perceive the total. And it is that insight that is the perception of the total. You get it? By Jove, I am working very hard. I wonder why? I don't want a thing from you—nothing! Thank God! Therefore I can talk because I want to.

So can the mind observe without the observer, which is thought? Can the mind observe the totality of fear? And when the mind is so capable of observing the totality of fear, is there fear? Do please look at it: the totality of fear, which means not only the conscious but also the unconscious fears—the totality. That means the mind is the totality—I don't know if you see this—not the totality of fear. The mind that is capable of look-ing at something wholly obviously has no fear.

You know when we talk about fear we must also go into the question of pleasure, enjoyment, joy, and a sense of beauty in which there is no demand for expression. You see most of us pur-sue and cultivate pleasure. We are not saying pleasure is right or wrong. We are just investigating, looking at it. Our philosophy, religion, social structure, and morality is based on pleasure, and the ultimate pleasure is God. Now, what is wrong with pleasure, which everybody wants? But if in the pursuit of pleasure there is no fulfillment, then what follows is pain, fear, violence, brutality. So the mind must find out both the nature of fear and of pleas-ure—the two dominant factors in our life.

What is pleasure? We have inquired sufficiently into fear. What is pleasure? Is it related to love? Is it related to enjoyment? Is it related to joy? Or is pleasure, the pursuit of it, the product of thought? Say I enjoy tremendously looking at a mountain: the delight, beauty, dignity, majesty of it, the glacier, the deep blue valleys and the straight-standing pines. I enjoy the whole beauty of it, looking out the window or from some height. There is a stimulation that brings a great delight. I go away from it, but the memory of that delight, of that mountain, remains. Then the memory, as thought, says, "I must go there tomorrow morning and look at it again." That is pleasure, isn't it? A delight that is natural, normal, healthy, sane, when pursued by thought, turns into pleasure that must be repeated, and when it is not repeated there is pain, frustration, and so on. So again there is an insight that thought breeds, gives a continuity to, pleasure as well as fear. The insight into that brings about an intelligent awareness of fear and pleasure, not the denial of one or the other. Are you fol-lowing all this? Am I saying too much at one go? Never mind. I must go on. Then what is joy? And is love pleasure, is love desire? There cannot be love if there is not the understanding of going beyond sorrow and the understanding of fear and pleasure. And what is joy? Can the mind invite joy? Or does it happen when you are not seeking it? And when it does happen, thought steps in and says, "I must have more of it," and therefore it becomes pleasure. See how extraordinary the whole thing is, what thought does. So love can be only when the other is not. Through negation you come to the positive. When there is the understanding of fear, of security, of sorrow, of the whole pursuit of endless pleasure, when you see the totality of all that, and go beyond it, then you know what love is.

Perhaps you would like to ask some questions.

QUESTIONER: How may one help another in a crisis?

KRISHNAMURTI: How may one help another in a crisis? I object most strenuously to the word *help*. Who am I to help you? Do listen to this carefully. You can help me in the kitchen, you can help me to drive a car. The questioner is not asking that. He says, "How can I help another in a crisis?" Who am I to help? Why do I think I can help? Please, I am asking this seriously, don't brush it aside. I say, "I can help you." Is it my vanity? Do I know more than you do? And if I do know more about the crisis than you do, can I help you to understand that crisis? I can only talk about it verbally. I can communicate verbally with you about the crisis, but can I help you to go beyond the crisis? Or do *you* have to do it? It sounds cruel.

So what am I to do when you are suffering? Crisis is some kind of sorrow, pain, fear. What am I to do to help, to help you to understand that crisis? That is the question, isn't it? What am I to do? Come on. I talk to you about it. It matters very much *how* I talk to you about it—sentimentally, emotionally, trying to comfort you. Does that help? So what shall I do? Give you my sympathy? Hold your hand? Does that help you to face the crisis? Can I give you so-called strength to face the crisis, cheer you up? What shall I do? Come on, please tell me. I am in sorrow, my son is dead, gone, or my husband, or whatever it is, what will you do with me? I am in tears, full of self-pity, a sense of loneliness, I feel I have lost everything that I had. You can hold my hand, give me a book to read that will give me comfort. Will that solve any of the problem for me?

All perhaps you can do is to be quiet, and if you love, if you know what it means to love, be in that quiet affectionate state. You can't do any more, can you? But to love is one of the greatest things in life. And to do that, to have that sense of compassion, passion, love, for everybody, you must understand, and know yourself—you who are in sorrow, self-centered activity, lonely, miserable, frightened—you are all that. If you understand yourself, you will have the wisdom that tells you how to deal with another. But don't, if I may suggest, start out wanting to help somebody. The missionaries want to help people. You ought to go to the countries of the East and see them. They do help people, only they bring other burdens with them for the people there to bear. They have their own burdens, their own gods, their own beliefs, so they bring another set of beliefs, another god. And so there begins a lot of misery and confusion.

Q: Is it because we do not have your insight that we ask you to do something we cannot do ourselves?

K: I have no insight. Who told you I have insight? I really mean it. Who has told you? We are sharing the insight together; it is not mine nor yours. Do please see this. It is not *my* insight I am sharing with you; it is insight for both of us. It is neither mine nor yours. It is insight, it is intelligence. If there is that intelligence between us, then we will do the right action, we will create a new world, new human beings, and so on.

Q: Could you please speak a little about the nature of indecision?

K: Could you please go into a little the nature of indecision, that is, not being able to decide. It is only a confused mind that wants to decide. Do you see that? If I am confused, I say, "I must do something." If I am clear, there is no decision, there is only action. It is only when I am uncertain what to do, what to think, how to act, that there must be choice. Then choice is based on my uncertainty, which is indecision, and being undecided then somebody or something decides, or I decide, to do something. So out of confusion you must have a choice of decisions. When there is clarity, there is no decision. Isn't it simple? It really is extraordinarily simple if you look at it, live with it.

I have never decided anything in my life—giving talks or not giving talks—nothing in my life. I didn't say, "I must give up property" or "I must do this" or "I must not do that." Never! There is beauty in that, because decision means will, doesn't it? I decide. Decision implies contradiction. Between two things you have to decide. Who is the entity that decides? Thought? Of course! But thought has created this division. Thought has created this uncertainty between whether I should do this or that.

Q: Is indecision not there at all?

K: Is indecision not there at all, the lady asks. Of course there is. I am pointing out that there is indecision only when there is no clarity. Look, I don't know how to get to Bern or Montreux. I don't know how to get there, so I ask. If I know, I don't ask. There is no decision; I take the road. Now, can my mind be so clear that there is no asking, deciding anything? I don't know—you follow? That is freedom, isn't it?

So can my mind, which is so confused, fragmented, and broken up, can that mind be completely clear? It can be clear only when I see the totality of my mind—the totality, not the various fragments of it, not putting together all the fragments to make a whole. When I see, when the mind sees, the total fragmentation, how these fragments are brought about, why they are in contradiction, I see nonanalytically—you can see all of that at one glance. You can do that only when the mind doesn't allow thought to come into it, when thought doesn't interfere in your observation, because thought is the entity, the factor, that brings about fragmentation.

# 6 ⑤ FEAR CAUSES ATTACHMENT TO BELIEF, DOGMA, PEOPLE, AND PROPERTY

WE HAVE BEEN TOGETHER talking over the whole nature of thought. And we ought also to explore, and try to discover for ourselves, what is the state of mind that is not afraid, that is not pursuing the demands of pleasure, that can enjoy without making joy into a pleasure; what is the quality of a mind that can understand, have an insight into the question of death; what it means to live totally; and also perhaps to come upon the question of what is love.

We have described in some detail how our brain and mind works, and how important it is to have complete security. It is only then that the brain can function normally, sanely, and healthily. We have said that the brain tries to find out if there is security in belief, in dogma, in conclusion. It hopes to find it in them, and so becomes terribly attached to them. And on discovering, if it is at all awake, that security, certainty, the quality of assurance, doesn't lie in any of them, it then tries to invent an illusion that is both intellectually and emotionally satisfactory. I don't know if you have observed this process going on all the time in our life:

Trying to find security and certainty in relationship, and not finding them there, it comes to a conclusion to which it becomes attached. And when that conclusion is questioned, disturbed, it runs away from it to another and then another conclusion, and gradually the mind begins to attach itself to things. So then there is attachment to property as well as to people or ideas.

As we grow older there is also the question of death, and I think we shall understand the deep meaning of that word if we can go into the question of attachment. Why the human mind, our mind, your mind, is attached to property, to people, to ideas—ideas being conclusions, opinions, traditions, a formula, which are all put together by thought, either in the form of an image, of a word that is a symbol, or of a nebulous, visionary illusion. Why is the mind attached to all these things? If you are not attached to an illusion or to a person, then you are attached to property, whether it is a house, a piece of land, or accumulated furniture. Why? What makes the mind, thought, cling to something like property, money? When we use the word *property*, it includes all that.

Why this clinging? Because, as we have said previously, mere inquiry into the causation doesn't free the mind from the cause. Intellectually, you can break down by analysis why the mind is attached to property, but at the end of it there is still attachment, which comes to an end only if we have an insight into the whole structure of attachment. Because to have an insight into something, to see the truth of something, brings its own freedom, brings its own intelligence. Now, why does the mind attach itself to property, to people and conclusions, ideas, symbols, visions, and all the rest of it? Why?

Attachment to property is not only to outer things but also includes attachment to one's own body, which is also a thing. And when we get attached to and safeguard a property, and later realize that it is not worth it, we then try to cultivate detachment. So there is attachment, then detachment, and then conflict between the two. Please, as we have said, you are not merely listening to a series of words, ideas, conclusions; we are sharing with each other, which implies listening and enjoying the thing that we are examining, because when you enjoy something you learn much quicker. I do not know if you have noticed this, but if you make a problem of something, you won't learn. To me it is very enjoyable, if I may use that word, to find out why my mind is attached to property. I want to learn about it, and am not therefore going to make a problem of it. If I make a problem of it, then I want to go beyond it, and the mind creates the idea of detachment. Then there is conflict between attachment and detachment, and the mind that is in conflict can never learn. It can learn the results of that conflict but not the root cause of attachment.

I do not know if you have gone into the question of enjoyment. There is a vast difference between pleasure and enjoyment. Pleasure has a motive. The pursuit of pleasure is the memory of a previous pleasure, and enjoyment is from moment to moment. You can't cultivate enjoyment, but you can cultivate pleasure. And when there is enjoyment, the brain relaxes. Watch it, and you will see. But when it is pursuing pleasure, it becomes tense, it becomes purposeful, and thought then cultivates determination, will. Whereas if there is enjoyment, all the brain cells relax. I was told the other day, by someone who seemed to know something about this, that scientists have recently discovered that when there is enjoyment a gland functions at the back of the head and makes the brain more active in a way that does not strain it.

So to learn there must be enjoyment. And you cannot enjoy, be happy, in the act of learning when you are comparing, judging, evaluating, or when you are storing up what you are learning in order to enjoy more. Please watch your own brain cells in operation! This is really a part of meditation: to observe completely without the act of will. When there is the act of will there is conflict. And what we are trying to do now—not "trying," sorry. What we are doing—I don't like the word *try*; when you try it means an effort. If you actually *do* it, it is going on. What we are trying to . . . —what we are *doing* is to observe happily why the mind is attached to property, because unless the brain cells, the mind, understands why there is attachment, death becomes a terror. Right? Why is the mind attached to so many things? Is it because there is nothing so permanent as property? There is the house, the furniture, the carpet, the picture, they are solid, and the mind can rest in and be attached to that solidity. Look at this, go into it fairly deeply, and you will see it for yourself.

Human relationship is uncertain. In it there is conflict, every form of struggle, jealousy, anxiety, fear, and pleasure, sexual or otherwise, companionship, and so on. And ideas too are rather uncertain, unclear, and property is the only thing that I can see that is solid.

QUESTIONER: It gets bombed so often it is not solid at all.

KRISHNAMURTI: Of course not, sir, but wait a minute. It has often been bombed, often destroyed, but human beings go back to it. You and I may say intellectually, "Well, property doesn't matter," but if we look into this very carefully, it doesn't matter what it is—one gets terribly attached to a pair of shoes. Perhaps those poor people in Vietnam may say that property doesn't matter, but it does matter, because otherwise they would have nothing.

So is that the reason the mind gets attached to property, whether mine or yours, or to the property of an institution with which it identifies as its property? And is it also because the mind needs to be occupied? It is never in a state of not being occupied. Please watch all this in yourself. And such occupation becomes extraordinarily important. A man goes to the office for forty, fifty, sixty years, and when being occupied with that comes to an end, he also comes to an end. So occupation becomes extraordinarily important, and the mind can be occupied with property, looking after it—you know all the business of owning something. So the mind needs to be occupied—whether it is with furniture, with social work, with a book, or with an idea of God, it is exactly the same—that it demands occupation. And is it also because the mind seems to have no existence in itself apart from the thing to which it is attached? What is the content of my mind, of my consciousness, or your consciousness? It is the property, the idea, the images that I have built about another or about myself. So the mind has no existence in itself apart from its content, and one of the contents is the furniture! And so it is not a question of being attached to it—furniture *is* the mind! And when the mind has no quality of itself, then attachment becomes extraordinarily important. Please observe this in yourself.

So the mind being lonely must have occupation, and the material existence of property and being occupied with that property take up a great deal of time in which one can be occupied. And the mind having no existence of its own finds existence in the content, in the attachment, in the idea.

And why are we so attached to people? Ah, this is much more interesting! Why are you attached to a person? Are you really attached to the person or to the idea, the image of that person? I am attached to you for various reasons: My attachment to you gives a quality, an existence to the mind, and my attachment to you is its existence. I am attached to you because I love you, you give me pleasure, sexual or otherwise; you give me something to which I can cling, companionship. An existence with you gives more certainty to the mind, and without you I am lost. And being lost, I have to find another companion, another attachment. Or if there is trouble between you and me—which is between the image I have of you and the image you have of me, which is called relationship—if there is conflict in that relationship, I try to break it up and establish another form of relationship, which is another image. Are you following all this?

So again I see that the mind, having no quality, vitality, existence, energy of its own, tries to find all that in relationship. Please watch this in yourself, not just listen to what the speaker is saying but actually look at what is going on in your mind when you are attached to a person, as obviously you must be when you call it love, with all its responsibility, all its neurotic behavior, and so on. Then there is this whole gamut of ideation, mentation. That is, the images that thought has created and put together as an idea, an idea being the reasoned-out, verbal assertion of a thought.

And we live on a formula, on conclusions, which are put together by thought, thought being memory and the past. So we are living in the past, which may be projected into the future, but our living still has its roots in the past. So our attachment is to the past. Now, why does the mind live, act, behave upon a series of conclusions that thought has come to? I don't know if you have noticed this in yourself. You have an experience—it doesn't matter what it is, however trivial, however great—and that experience becomes the memory of it, and that memory with its knowledge is the process of thought, which comes to a conclusion, and according to that conclusion you live. The conclusion is nonphysical, nonexistent; it is still an idea. And the mind, having no vitality of its own, has to depend on ideas, formulas, beliefs, doctrines, and all the rest of it, and therefore there is constant division between the conclusion and act. Are we all asleep?

So I see the mind is its content. It does not exist without its content. And it is afraid to let go of its content, otherwise it has no existence. And so it has got to occupy itself with its content: the furniture, people, the person or idea, idea being God, you know all the rest of it. You see how extraordinarily interesting it is, because meditation, what they *call* meditation, is cultivating an occupation with an idea, and the practicing of that idea, which is not meditation at all—we'll discuss that perhaps later—but see how the whole thing hangs together like a marvelous structure.

Now, one has explained all this: the attachment to property, attachment to people, to conclusions, to your images, symbols, ideas. To have an insight into that, into the whole of it, is liberation from attachment, not at some future date but instantly. This is really important to understand. When you listen to this, do you say, "I will think about this and go into this much more later; because too many ideas are being poured out here, I must take it up and think about it later"?—which prevents you from having an insight now. If we are sharing this thing together, there is no time for you to think about it later.

We are sharing this food together because you are hungry, and the speaker is also hungry; we are eating the food together. You don't say when you are eating together, or when you are hungry, "I will eat later"—you are sharing it, actively eating. And if you have no insight into what has been said . . . why? Are you frightened of not being attached, of not being occupied, of what happens to a mind that has no attachment? Because when the mind is incessantly occupied, whether with your house, sex, God, drink, politics, or guru, that gives it a vitality, a certain quality of energy. And one is afraid of what will take place if there is no occupation at all. So when there is fear of that, you will not share; the fear will prevent you.

You need therefore to have an insight into that fear, which is far more important than to have an insight into attachment. And when you have such insight, attachment goes altogether, and a different quality comes into being, the quality that the mind itself has when it has understood, is aware of, and has had an insight into the whole process of attachment. That is love. How can I love you, or you love me, if I am attached to you? My attachment is based on my pursuit of pleasure, which you give me, the image of you and so on. I am attached to that image of you, and you are attached to the image of me. And the image is the past, is the response of experience, knowledge. So is love the past? Is love experience? Is love memory? Is love the reaction to that memory as pleasure?

So one discovers, or the mind comes upon the fact, that where there is attachment of any kind there is no love. This is not a statement, an idea, but an actual fact that the mind has discovered, which the mind, having an insight into attachment, sees the truth of. And seeing the truth of it, it is not occupied with the person, or with the furniture, or with the idea, and therefore it has its own energy. It is that quality of energy that is love, right? And therefore love can never be hurt—oh, you don't see all this, do you? Love can never be jealous, never lonely, never ask to be loved—what a horror that is!

And one observes what one's life is. What is our life? What is our existence? Look at it, please. Your existence, not mine. Which means, What is the existence of the "me" in the field of knowledge? What is my living in the field of experience? What is my actual activity with the whole structure of memory, which is the past? Is my life based on the past—the past being yesterday, or ten thousand yesterdays? Please look at it. I want to learn about myself, and I have learned happily what my attachments do to the mind, and I want to find out also what my actual life is, not my imagined life, not the life I would like to have, not the life that depends on environment, on stimuli, but actually what my daily existence is based on. Am I living in the past, is my life the past, operating, reacting to the present based upon the past and therefore projecting that to the future? I want to find out—please listen to this carefully. I want to find out. I want to find out whether temperament and idiosyncrasy are my life, or is my life my conditioned state, or are temperament, idiosyncrasy, and conditioning my whole life? Am I making this complex?

What is temperament? What is idiosyncrasy? You have a certain temperament and certain idiosyncrasies, haven't you? According to the dictionary, temperament is, as far as one can make out, based on experience, and idiosyncrasy is something that is put together. We all have various kinds of idiosyncrasy and temperament and their activity, but basically we are all conditioned, though the temperament and idiosyncrasy may vary from person to person. You and I are basically and deeply conditioned according to the culture, to the past, to all of that, conditioned consciously or unconsciously through heredity, tradition, through a thousand years of human struggle. And also according to time, climate, culture, which vary the expression of idiosyncrasy and temperament. That is, you are different in temperament from me. You have idiosyncrasies different from mine. And we try to balance these idiosyncrasies and temperaments and to bring harmony between us, which can never be done; whereas harmony between us exists, can come, only when the mind has an insight into the total conditioning.

Shall we take a breather for a minute? Because this is really quite important and rather interesting if you go into it. You see, we are trying to bring harmony outwardly in relationship between temperaments and idiosyncrasies. But inwardly we are deeply conditioned, and we try to somehow live together with our absurd idiosyncrasies and temperaments, and in that there is always battle, strife. I am trying to adjust myself to your temperament, and you are trying to adjust to my idiosyncrasies, aren't you? This is what is going on in life. And there is this constant effort, battle, and I say to myself, "This is totally wrong somehow, it has no value." Because your temperament and idiosyncrasies can vary, change, and so character has no value. But what does have significance is to find out, to have an insight into this whole conditioning. Then if the mind is free from the conditioning that is its content, our relationship is entirely different;

there is no conflict between you and me because it is not based on pleasure and all the rest of it.

Now, can the mind see, have an insight into, this whole business of conditioning, temperament, idiosyncrasy, how the mind is the result of the past, of evolution? Not tomorrow, but now, instantly, have insight into ourselves, and therefore that insight brings its own energy to transform *what is*. Insight has its own tremendous energy, which is not dependent on any stimuli, and therefore it transforms what is observed, which is attachment. Have you got that insight, and therefore that tremendous energy to actually change your attachment totally? So that the mind doesn't derive its energy from attachment, from conflict, and all that, but has its own vital energy, independent of environment, of culture, of people? Come on! Then living means something quite different from the way we live now, which is in conflict.

Then we have to inquire into the whole question of what is death. Do you mind inquiring into that? There are a lot of young people here who may live a very long time, and there are a lot of old people too, including myself. We are the people who are going, and you are the people who are coming. But whether going or coming, you have to face death. So we are going to inquire into it, which means we are going to have an insight into it. And you cannot have that insight if there is any kind of fear, and fear comes only when you are attached to the things that are known, the things known being your images, your knowledge, furniture, opinions, judgments, culture, your shyness, your politeness—all that is the field of the known. And if you are afraid you will never have an insight into the whole problem of death.

I want to find out, as you must, what is death. Why am I frightened of it? Why am I so scared of old age and suddenly coming to an end? To wholly understand death is really a very complex business. And the very complexity of it makes one frightened. It is like very complex machinery, you daren't touch it, because you know nothing about it. But if you approach it very simply, which means you are really trying to learn about it, and are therefore enjoying that—not the idea of death but enjoying the investigation, the approach, the inquiry—then you learn. And you cannot learn if you are unhappy or frightened. That is a basic thing.

So if you really want to go into this, you have to be very clear that your mind, which means your thought, doesn't create fear of what it considers to be coming to an end, what it considers to be entering into something it doesn't know.

I don't know where to begin this. Fear being totally out of the picture, first of all I have to find out, I want to find out, if there is anything permanent as the "me." Permanent, that is, which has a continuity. I can leave my furniture to my brother, son, or whoever, and therefore it can remain in the family, or be sold to somebody else in an antique shop, but I want to find out if there is anything substantial, continuous, permanent as the "me" who is frightened of death.

Is there anything permanent in me, in you—permanent in the sense of having a continuity in time, a duration in space as the "me"? The "me" is the name, right? Has that name any permanency? Or is it that thought gives permanency to the name? In itself it has no permanency, but thought, by identifying itself with the body, the image, the knowledge, with all the experiences, sorrows, pleasures, agonies, by identifying itself with all that, gives it a quality of permanency. Otherwise is there anything permanent, a thing that has continuity in spite of the nonexistence of the body? Are you interested in all this? You are going to face this, whether you like it or not. You are going to face it either accidentally, or through disease or the natural decay of the organism. It is inevitable. You can avoid it by living longer, in a healthier way, taking more pills, and so forth—you know, carry on. But at the end there is this fact.

I must find out for myself if there is something permanent beyond death—permanent meaning timeless, which cannot be corrupted through civilization, through culture, something that in spite of all experience, knowledge, stimuli, reactions has its own existence and goes on as the "me." So man has said, "There is not the 'me,' but there is God"—follow all this carefully. In Asia, in India, they put it differently, but it is still the act of thought that says, "There is Brahman." It is an act of thought that says, "There is the soul." It is thought that is frightened of the unknown, because thought *is* the known, thought is time, thought is the old, thought is never free.

Thought is the response of memory, experience, knowledge, and so it is always old, never free; and being of time it is uncertain of the timeless, of that which is beyond time. So it says, "I am not important; the 'me' is transient, has been put together by time, by accident, by the family, by tradition, by the culture in which it has been put together; it has developed certain tendencies, idiosyncrasies; it has its conditioning, but beyond all that there is the soul, there is something immense in me that is the permanent." All that is the process of thought. And thought, when confronted with the inevitable, which is death, the ending, says, "I can't tolerate this." So it says, "There must be a future life" or "I believe there is a future life" or "There is heaven and I'll sit next to God"—it wants comfort when faced with something completely unknown. And there are thousands of people who will give you that comfort. All the organized churches offer it, and you want it, and therefore they exist.

Now, if you say, "How do I find out about all this?" it is still the action of thought, and therefore based on fear, on imagination, on the past. That is, the field of the known, which is, "I am attached to the field of the known, with all its varieties, changes, its activities, and what I demand is comfort, and because I have found comfort in the past, I have lived within the field of the known. That is my territory, I know its borders, its frontiers—the frontiers are my consciousness, which is its content. I am completely familiar with all that, and death is something I don't know, I don't want."

So my life has been the past, I live in the past, I act in the past; that is my life. Listen to this: My life that is living in the past is a dead life; my mind that lives in the past is a dead mind; but thought says, "That is not death, the future is death." So I see this as a fact, I see this as something enormously real. Therefore the mind, realizing that, actually dies to the past. It will use the past, but the past has lost its grip, its values, its vitality. So the mind has its own energy, which is not derived from the past. Therefore living is dying. Therefore living is love, which is dying. Because if there is no attachment, then there is love. If there is no attachment to the past, the past has its value that can and must be used as knowledge, but my living is then a constant renewal, a constant movement in the field of the unknown in which there is learning, moving. Therefore death is the ultimate aloneness. And so there is a totally different kind of life.

Sorry, I've talked for a long time. Now, there was the gentleman who had questions.

QUESTIONER: Does there not have to be a giving up or surrendering of ourselves?

KRISHNAMURTI: Ah, I didn't use the words *giving up* or *surrendering*. I said the mind, consciousness, is its content. Its content is the books, the television, the amusements, furniture, and so on—all the content that civilization and culture have put into it. And if you say you must be unattached, that is an act of will by thought, in which there is therefore no freedom. But if you have an insight into this, then it is total.

Q: Is it not blind faith to accept that there is such a different quality of mind?

K: The questioner asks, Is it not blind faith to accept that there is such a different quality of mind? How can you accept what another says? How can you have faith in what somebody else says? He may be mistaken, he may be trying to convert you to some idiocy, and all conversion is idiocy. But what he says to you is, Look at it yourself, learn about it for yourself, have an insight into this whole process for yourself. So there is no authority. You don't have to have faith in something, in a belief, or in a person.

Q: How do images convey real feelings though I know they are dead?

K: How do images convey real feelings though I know they are dead? Look, I have images that are put together by thought, put together through experience, through reactions, through various crises. Those images are real because I accept them intellectually as being real. The intellect, which is part of thought, lives with and derives energy from those images, and therefore they have a life of their own. They give you vitality, they give you feeling, they maintain you, nourish you, but though the intellect may say that such nourishment, such maintenance, those stimuli are false, are unreal, unless you have deep awareness and an insight into the machinery that makes the images, these images will go on giving you neurotic reactions. Every form of image that you have is bound to create a neurotic reaction and neurotic feelings.

Q: Sir, during dreamless sleep there is no image. I would like to know if fragmentation and images are necessary in order to have an insight into them.

K: Dreamless sleep is a state of mind in which there are no images, no conditioning, no time. Now, are you telling me that, or have you heard somebody else tell you that?

Q: I think it is obvious.

K: The gentleman says, "I think it is obvious." Sir, the mountain is obvious, the beauty, the majesty, the height of it is obvious, but I have to climb it, I have to live with it, I have to move with it. What is obvious is not necessarily real. What is real is to see if I have images, to see if the mind derives energy from those images, and to see in my everyday life whether these images play a part in my relationship. And what my day is, my night is. The movement of my daily life continues in dreams when I sleep. To have no dreams at all is one of the most important things because when the mind sleeps, when it is in a state of absolute quietness, then it rejuvenates. But if it is a continuity of the day then it is struggling, and the struggle is to bring order. I don't know if you have noticed this. The brain can function normally, healthily, nonneurotically only when it has no image, is not in conflict, and has complete order. But if during the day you have no order, then it tries to establish order during the night, which is part of the dream.

So if being aware during the day, you are trying to find out and to learn, and there is learning, insight, enjoying the insight, then during the night the mind that has established order during the day can sleep completely without dreaming at all, and therefore has quite a different movement, quite a different vitality.

Q: I have a problem. Sometimes in life it seems to me that you have to be egotistic to go the way you are talking about, because you have to change your relationships and sometimes people hurt you and sometimes you hurt them very much. What is the answer?

K: Sometimes in life, the questioner says, you have to be selfish. You may hurt others in that selfishness and they may hurt you. What is the answer? Is that the question?

Q: You have to be egotistic to go the way of freedom.

K: You have to be egotistic to be free. I think we are misusing, or misunderstanding each other in the use of, that word *egotistic*. I see something that is true, not because of my temperament or my idiosyncrasy or my conditioning; I see something to be real, to be factual. Now, wait a minute, I'll show it to you. I see that to belong psychologically to any group, to hold any belief, is destructive, and I don't belong to any group, to any organization. You will call me very selfish, won't you? Because you think I am having my own way, I am following my idiosyncrasy, my particular character, and so you call me selfish. Am I, because I see something to be true?

Suppose, for instance, that I see nationalism to be a poison. So I say, "I don't belong to any nation," and you say to me, "You are very selfish in following your particular opinion," because you live in opinion, and you think that I am also acting according to opinion. I am not. I see that it is a danger, as I see a snake to be a danger. If you don't see it as a danger, and I do, why call me egotistic? I am not. So the mind must be very clear that it is not acting on idiosyncrasy, temperament, experience, but is being aware, having an insight—which has nothing whatsoever to do with the past, with my egotism.

Q: Can you go into the question of words and concepts, and the problems they cause in communication inside and outside oneself?

K: Words are necessary to communicate. There are other forms of communication, but we will take words first. If I want to tell you something, I must use words, a gesture, or a look. So words become important in communication, that is, if we both speak the same language. And words become important if we both give a word the same meaning. If I call that microphone an elephant, that is meaningless. So words have a meaning because they have a common referent between you and me. And words are also a danger because words are used to convey thoughts: I am thinking one thing, I put it into words and convey it to you. And if my thought is crooked, not clear, I use words that are clear to you but are therefore deceptive. Or I want to deceive you, consciously or unconsciously.

Words are put together by thought and are necessary, and are there other means of communication apart from words? Can you read my thought without that thought being put into words? Obviously that can be done and is done. When two people are fairly friendly, fairly sympathetic, fairly interested in the same thing, they can communicate very quickly without words. And are there other means of communication beyond the word and thought? I can convey to you that those bells are ringing and it is twelve o'clock. I am using words because you are also listening to that bell. Also I can communicate with you through a gesture, through a look. And must thought always be expressed in words, or is there thought without the word? Then what am I communicating with you?

Is love a word? Is love a thought? Is love a sentiment? If the word is not the thing, then how do I communicate the thing to you without the word, without the gesture, without holding your hand, and so on? How do I communicate that love, which is not the word, to you who are used to the word, when to you the word has become tremendously important? I have to keep on telling you, "I love you, I love you, I love you." If I don't use the word and I have that thing called love, then how is it communicated? It can be communicated to you only if we are together at the same time, at the same level, at the same intensity. Then there is communication without the word. But naturally to us the word is very important. And that word can be misunderstood, and so on. But there are qualities, states, certain facts that are incommunicable through words.

# 7 ✿ LIVING RELIGIOUSLY

W E HAVE TALKED ABOUT so many things during the
last six talks, and I would like now, if I may, to talk
with you on the question of religion, what is meditation, and try to come upon something that may be not of a visionary nature, not therefore visions or "experiences," but an
actual dimension that thought cannot possibly enter.

I do not know if you have noticed that most of our lives are
rather boring, tiresome, with very little meaning in themselves.
We try to give meaning, intellectual meaning, to our existence,
but that too has very little significance. And we may try to enrich
our lives by studying or inquiring into occultism or witchcraft—
that I believe is the fashion now, which is as old as the hills, and
not very serious either—or by indulging in various forms of dis-
traction. Because the way our lives are lived is rather narrow, rep-
etitious, tiresome, fearful, anxious, and so on. So when we talk
about religion, it becomes an escape rather than an actuality. So
if we can this morning, we should share together an inquiry into
what actually is religion, a religious life, a religious mind, a religious way of existence.

Obviously, we should, if we can, put aside all the organized religions with their beliefs and dogmas, with their priests, their structure that thought has put together, because in themselves they have no validity, except for what man has invented, except for what a few have experienced, and assert that this is so or that is not.

What is a religious mind? What is a religious way of living? I think we should go into this, because it is a vital question, like love, like death, sorrow, and human relationship; it is as important as, perhaps, if not more important than all of these to find out for oneself what it is to live a life that is truly and deeply religious. The word *religion* means—I looked it up the other day in the dictionary—"tie together." And the word *yoga*—perhaps most of you know that word—also means "joined together," like two yoked oxen. So in the ordinary dictionary meaning, *religion* and *yoga* imply the same thing, that is, bring together, tie together, yoke the higher part to the lower part, the spirit and matter, and so on.

First of all, that implies division. When you say bring together, join together, tie together, this implies that there is a division in existence. Why is it that we have divided life into a religious and nonreligious life, spirit and matter, the higher and the lower; why is there such fragmentation in our existence? There is the mind, the heart, and the body. And this division has existed throughout the ages. We don't treat existence as a whole. We treat it as a thing that is divided and must be brought together. The bringing together implies, doesn't it, an outside agency or an agency in yourself. Please follow this a little, if you're interested in it. And we are sharing this together. It implies an outside agency that will bring the divided, fragmented existence together, through a religious activity, through yoga, through meditation, through various forms of exercise, control, and so on.

Now, is there such a division? Or has thought divided existence, life, as separate from the higher state of thought? Thought has obviously invented the higher state, hasn't it? The soul, the Hindus call it the *atman*, and so on. Thought has brought this about. So thought is responsible for this division. And, not being able to bring this together, not being able to bring about a total harmony, it then invents a superior entity that is going to integrate the various fragments. Now, that integrating factor is called God, an outside agency, or your own will, and so on.

One can see that one needs a total harmony, that is, a harmony of the mind, the intellect, the capacity to reason logically, sanely; and of the heart, the capacity to have compassion, love, kindliness, consideration; and of the physical, with all its complexities. One can see that there must be such harmony. Because only then can existence function healthily and totally.

And we are asking, Can religion that is based on belief, on an insight of the few who have established a church, an organized priesthood, and so on, can such a structure bring about harmony in you? Or is it that such harmony has nothing whatsoever to do with belief, with any savior, with any guru, with any sense of an outside agency, or an inward effort to bring about harmony? Am I making myself clear? You look rather puzzled. All right, I'll put it this way.

I see for myself that the mind, with the brain, can function only when there is complete inner harmony—total harmony, not fragmentary harmony. Now, how is this to be brought about? I don't know how, but people say, religions say, authority asserts, that there must be an agency outside of you: God, whatever name you like to give to it. And if you could concentrate on that, give your life to that, believe in that, perhaps you can bring about this extraordinary quality of harmony. They don't put it this way, I'm putting it this way.

Now, belief is conceived by thought. Belief is the result of thought and fear. I see that, so I reject totally all belief and therefore all authority. There's no guru, no teacher, no savior, nobody outside that can bring about this extraordinary state of harmony. And I realize harmony is not integration of the various fragments. To bring about integration, that is, to put together the various broken parts, implies there must be an entity who, through an act of will, desire, or urgency, can bring this integration about. That again is a fragmentation. Are you following all this? So I reject that too. I reject belief, I reject authority, the whole structure of a religious organization based on authority—all that goes. Then how am I, how is the mind, to bring about this harmony? Because I see that it is essential in order to be healthy, to have tremendous energy, and to have a mind that is extraordinarily clear. Now, is harmony a thing to be cultivated? Cultivation implies time, doesn't it? I need time to cultivate a plant.

Give your mind to this a little. Please share this with me. So I say I need time to cultivate this harmony, either through various forms of mental or physical exercise or through control. Or I set a course and follow that course, which is the action of will. I see that the mind, the brain, and the heart, and the physical entity, can function beautifully, easily, smoothly, when there is a complete sense of the whole in which there is no division. I see that very clearly. First I see it perhaps intellectually, verbally, and I realize that that has no value. Then how does the mind bring this about? Does this question mean anything to you? Because this is the religious life, not belief or disbelief in God or gods, or having your own various visions and "experiences"—to me that is not a religious life. So I have to be very clear, I have to find out what it means to live a religious life. Because I feel if that can be brought about, or comes into being, then my action at any level will always be harmonious and noncontradictory.

So my mind has rejected the whole structure of belief, which is based on fear and therefore illusion. Please, you're sharing this with me, we are walking together, thinking together, creating together, and therefore establishing between ourselves right communication. And so I reject also, completely, any authority, because it is still outside myself, it is still the act of thought that seeks guidance from another. That brings about division, and hence conflict—what I should do according to what another says, and trying to conform to the pattern set by another. So that brings about conflict and therefore disharmony. Are you following all this?

Then, I ask myself, will any act of desire, which is will, bring this about? Because will plays a great part in our life. Will is based on choice, on decision: I will do this, and I will not do that. Will, that is, the concentration of desire, plays an extraordinary part in our life. Haven't you noticed it? I must do this, I must not do that, I will follow this course. And such constant decision making is part of our existence. And I see that where there is the act of will, there must be division and therefore conflict. And where there is conflict, there can be no harmony. So is there a way of living without the action of will? As I said, will comes into being when there is choice. And choice exists when there is confusion. And you do not choose, you do not decide, when you see things very clearly. Then you act, and this is not the action of will.

So I am asking myself, Why is it that my mind cannot see clearly, function clearly all the time, not just occasionally? Why do you think your mind doesn't function clearly? First of all, it is confused. It is confused because its past conditioning meets the present, and is incapable of understanding the present, and life being so uncertain, people assert this, the authorities assert that, work for this, don't work for that, this is true, that is false; there are a dozen experts or gurus telling you what to do—and we're caught in all that.

Also, confusion exists because we *want* clarity; we want to reach the other shore where we think there is clarity. So we are always making life, which is this shore, into a problem, because we want to get over there, where we think we're going to be perfectly happy, sitting next to God, or entering nirvana, or achieving liberation, or whatever. So the other shore makes the problem. And that is one of the causes of confusion. I wonder if you follow all this?

So I have an insight, there is an insight, into this question of the action of will. Have you got that insight, as we are talking? Then there is no conflict in the mind; it acts when there is insight. Action is insight, not the action of will, or belief, or fear, or greed; insight that comes when you observe very closely this pattern of existence established by will. When you have an insight into that, your action is entirely different, and therefore noncontradictory, and hence that insight brings harmony. The reason I have no insight is that I live in the past. Your life is the past, isn't it? Your remembrances, your imaginings, your contriving are based on the past. So our life is the past, which through the present, modified, becomes the future. So as long as you live in the past, there must be a contradiction, and hence conflict.

So harmony comes into being when you have insight into all this. However, we are educated to control ourselves. Or, having been educated in the structure of control, you discard all that and go to the other extreme, which is also happening. And again control implies division, right? The controller and the thing controlled. The controller says, "This must happen, I must do this, I must not get angry, I must be this." So there is a controller and the thing he's trying to control, and hence a division. Is the controller different from the thing he's controlling? Or are they both the same? Of course they are the same. And not being able to go beyond the thing controlled, thought invents a controller and hopes thereby to go beyond that which he is trying to control. Do you get all this? I am angry, and I say, "I must not be angry." That is, instantly there is a division. But the entity that says, "I must not be angry" is part of anger, otherwise you couldn't recognize the anger. Therefore the controller is the controlled. When I have an insight into the division that exists when there is an act of will through control, and the strife there must be in that division, a totally different kind of action comes about that is not controlled or under any restraint.

Is all this becoming too much? Anyhow, this is the last talk. Now, see what my mind has done: I have an insight into belief, I have an insight into will, I have an insight into control, authority, measurement. That is our cultural background, the basis of our religious, ethical, moral, and social background. And when I have an insight into that, there is the cessation of it all. When I see something false, when there is perception of something as dangerous, it is dropped, you run away from it. It is the false, the untrue, that creates disharmony.

Then mind wants to find out if there is something more than mere thought and its structure. Man throughout the ages has sought this. He has inquired into the known and is always adding more to its extent through more knowledge, more technology, better means of communication, new ways of reducing pollution, you know all that is going on within the field of the known, including your gods, saviors, masters, gurus, enlightenment. All that is within the field of the known, which is the function of thought.

Are we communicating with each other? You see, thought is measurement, right? Because to measure means according to the known, according to memory, according to experience. So there are people who say, "You must meditate to find out if there is something beyond the known." And they say, "Control your thought, discipline your thought, become aware of your thought," so they are still dealing with thought, control by thought, discipline by thought. And through thought they hope to find the thing that is not measurable. And people also say, "You must stop thinking, kill the mind." So now we are going to find out.

I said at the beginning that we were going to talk this morning about religion and meditation and, if this is possible, come upon something that is not measurable but of a totally different dimension. We have talked somewhat about religion. Now we are going to find out what it means to meditate. I don't know what it means to you. If you had never heard that word, if you had never heard any of the experts telling you how to meditate, it would be much better, because then the two of us could investigate it together, not knowing. But if you know what it is already, then that becomes a burden, a block, right?

So I want to find out what it means to a mind that is capable of meditation. The dictionary says the word means "to ponder over, to be concerned with, to have an intellectual, an emotional grasp," and so on. That is the dictionary meaning.

There are also the various meanings that all the religions have given to it; in the West it may be called contemplation, and in the East they prefer meditation. And I want to find out as a human being, because I don't belong to the East or the West, I'm neither a Zen follower nor a Krishnamurti follower. I don't know, and I've no external authority because I've no guru, thank God! So I want to find out what it means to meditate. But I can see one thing very clearly, which is that as long as thought is functioning, it must function according to the past and project itself into the future—from the known to the known. I see that very clearly. As long as thought is operating, nothing new can take place. Be clear on this. Because thought is based on the past, thought is the reaction of memory, thought is the outcome of the knowledge, the experience that is my background. So thought is old, it can never bring about freedom, because it is not in itself free. I see that very clearly. Nobody has to convince me of it.

So I see, the mind perceives, that as long as there is the movement of thought, it is living in the old and is incapable of perceiving something totally new. Please don't be convinced by me, by the speaker—observe it for yourself. Thought has invented the whole structure of the religious way of life—rituals, monks, nuns, priests, the authority of the priesthood, the whole structure. And what they say is still within the pattern of thought. Therefore I have an insight into the whole process of thinking and the illusions that it can create.

I see that there must be the emptying of the known. That is, thought must function at one level, because otherwise I can't do anything, but if we are to inquire and come upon something immeasurable—if there is something immeasurable—thought must be completely still. Only then can I see something new. The seeing of something new is creation—not my painting, writing a book, or doing some silly thing, because that is still within the pattern of the known, within the pattern of thought, with its imagination, contrivance, remembrance. So I see the mind must be completely quiet—not that it must be *made* quiet—for then who is the entity that is going to make it quiet? That entity is the desire that wishes to have a mind that is quiet, and so there is a division in that and hence conflict and disharmony. So how is the mind to be absolutely quiet, which means the brain cells themselves? Brain cells hold the memories, and if they are healthy, these memories will react healthily. If they are not healthy, neurotic action takes place, or one is caught in illusions.

So the brain must be quiet, but active when demanded. So there is this problem of having a very quiet, extraordinarily subtle, pliable, quick, sensitive mind that is free of the known and yet functions in the field of the known. The two must go together all the time, otherwise there is disharmony. So how is this to happen? One can see very clearly that knowledge, memory, experience are absolutely necessary, otherwise you couldn't talk. But it becomes a danger when thought, in its desire to be secure, uses knowledge for its own self-centered activity. So one must be aware of that.

Now, how is the mind to be quiet? Is there a system, a method? Now, look at it. If there is a system established by you or by another—a system being a method, a practice, and the daily practicing of that system to make the mind quiet—who is the entity that is practicing the system? That entity is thought, which says, "If I could practice this method, this system, then I will have a quiet mind, and it must be a marvelous state. I want to experience that state." So thought invents its own system or accepts another's system, in order to experience something totally new, in which thought can take pleasure. So that becomes a problem.

So the mind has to find out why there is this constant demand for experience. Why do you want experience, any kind of experience? Either you have it directly or indirectly, by reading novels or watching television. Why do you want experience? Have you ever gone into that question? There is sexual experience, there is experience of so many kinds—why does the mind demand it? Because you're bored with the routine and mechanical nature of everyday experience. And you want to experience something that is nonmechanical, right? And you set about it through a mechanical means, which is thought, and through a mechanical means you hope to experience something that is nonmechanical. And if you do experience it, then it becomes mechanical, because thought has invented that experience. So the mind says, I don't want any experience. I see its value, I need experience when acquiring knowledge in everyday life, and the more experience I have in putting machinery together, the more I can bring about a way of living that will be mechanical, right?

So the mind says, Any demand for experience, high or low, noble or ignoble, is still part of thought, which wants to experience something in which it can take pleasure. You don't want to experience ugly things, painful things; you only want to experience pleasurable things, and God of course is the ultimate pleasure. So seeing that, the mind no longer asks for any kind of experience, and so there is no illusion. The moment the mind wants to experience something great, it can invent that greatness, it can invent something that it calls enlightenment. But if all that ceases, what is the state of the mind that doesn't demand experience? At present you need experience to keep you awake. But having insight into all that, the mind doesn't need an experience to keep it awake: It is awake.

Now we're asking, Can the mind and the brain be completely still? And you want to know if it is still, don't you? I want to know if my mind is still. And in America there is a gadget called Alpha Meditation that will tell you by electronic measurement whether your mind is still. Americans are good at gadgetry. I can be silly, stupid, dull, illogical in daily existence, and I wire this instrument to my head, and it tells me when I'm quiet.

So Zen, all these forms of meditation like mantra yoga, the repetition of words, all those are means of knowing for yourself that your mind is quiet. Can you know your mind is quiet? Please do think it out. If you know your mind is quiet, then there is no quietness because there is you observing the mind you think is quiet. So you cannot experience a mind that is quiet—see the beauty of it—any more than you can experience happiness or joy. The moment you say, "I am joyful," it is gone. The moment you say, "How happy I am!" it ends. So the mind, when it is quiet, has no observer. Are you learning all this? As I have said, you can learn when you are happy, not when you make a problem of it. And the problem only exists when you want to have a quiet mind. But when you are happy and want to learn what it means to have a quiet mind, you find that a quiet mind comes into being when there is no observer, no experiencer, no thinker. But, you will, say, "How am I to stop the thinker from acting?" You can't stop it, but you can learn about the whole nature, the workings and the movement of thought, learn it. And when you do that, the other comes into being.

It does so when the brain and the mind and the body are absolutely quiet, that is, when there is no entity that is all the time measuring, comparing: "I have had this experience yesterday, and I'd like to have more." All of which is measurement.

Quietness implies space, doesn't it? Have you noticed how little space one has both outwardly and inwardly in oneself? When you live in a city, in a small flat surrounded by other flats, and across the street there is another block, so that you are living in a small, enclosed space outwardly, you want to break things, don't you? That is part of our violence, not only the violence inherited from the aggressive animal that we are, but the violence from this enclosed living in towns with very little outward space. So you take three weeks' holiday once a year. My God, what a way to live! Your whole body revolts with this constant going to the office for forty years of your life, all enclosed, in close contact with each other. Have you ever noticed in the evening when birds are sitting on a telephone wire? They have regular space between them, which they demand, which they must have. But we don't want space, we want to be close together, because we are frightened to be alone.

We also lack space emotionally, because we are attached—I must be with that person, I can't bear to be alone, I must have companionship, I must be occupied. So inwardly and outwardly we have very little space and therefore become more and more violent, or escape from it altogether, through sectarian attitudes, various religious organizations, following bearded gurus, and so on—escaping.

And space is an extension in which there are objects and no objects. Now, for most of us, our minds are filled with things. Thoughts are also things, not only furniture and books and knowledge. So inwardly we have very little space, and in that little space there is the movement of occupation, self-centered occupation, or the movement is outward but it is still occupation from the center.

So the mind that is absolutely quiet has space without any

object in it. The moment there is an object, that object creates space around itself, and therefore there is no other space. The moment there is in one's mind an object—a chair, a belief, fear, the persistent demand for pleasure, objects—then each object creates its own little space around itself. And we try to expand these little spaces, hoping to capture the great space. I wonder if you are meeting all this. So the mind that is completely quiet has space in which there is no object, and therefore an attention not about or to something, but simply a state of attention. And if you notice, when there is attention, there is extraordinary space. It is only when there is inattention that the object becomes important. So attention is not a matter of cultivation, going to a school to learn how to be attentive, going to Japan or India or some Himalayan town and learning to be attentive, which is all so manifestly silly, but attention is this extraordinary sense of space. And that cannot exist when the mind is not completely quiet. And this quietness is total harmony.

Then the mind is not dissipating energy. Now, we dissipate energy in quarrels, in gossip, in fighting each other, in dozens of ways! And we need tremendous energy to transform *what is*. *What is* is your anger, your ambition, your greed, your envy, desire for power, position, and prestige. To go beyond *what is*, you need tremendous energy. But you have no energy if you are battling with *what is*.

So life is a movement in harmony when there is this energy that has gone beyond *what is*. Because attention is the concentration of total energy. And all this is meditation. And one asks, Is there something beyond all thought, something that is immeasurable, not nameable, that no words can describe? Is there something like that? How are you going to find out? Will you accept what another says? Will you put your faith in the words or the experience of another? If you put your faith in another, do you know what happens to you? You are destroyed, because the other fellow becomes all-important. So as you cannot put your faith in anything or in anybody, there is freedom. And when there is freedom, the mind, which has dissipated its energy through struggle, conflict, and the pursuit of pleasure, the mind itself becomes extraordinarily full of energy without any outward stimuli. Only in that state is there something that is not measurable and is not nameable. And nobody can convey it to you.

Do you want to ask any questions?

QUESTIONER: How does one go about finding what one loves to do, instead of just accepting an adequate job?

KRISHNAMURTI: As things are now politically, economically, with all the social injustices, you can't find a job that you love. Is that it? That is, if you are an artist you say, "I love what I am doing." If you are an artist you might love painting, writing a poem, or shaping marble or clay. But you will still depend for your livelihood on another; you have to sell your pictures, your poems. You have to accept others' saying whether your poem is good or not, worth publishing or not, is saleable or not. So you depend on society.

If you become a monk, you also depend. So with society, culture, the world's economic structure being as they are, how will you find, a job you really love, and how will you be able to live? Is that the question? The questioner says, "I want to find a job that I really love." Is that the issue, or will you accept any job because you are not emotionally and psychologically dependent on it? That is, most of us are seeking status through a job. We don't want to remain a cook, we want to become the chef, because the chef has status. We don't want to be merely a priest, we want to become a bishop, then an archbishop, and finally the Pope, because that has immense prestige. So what most of us are concerned with is not function but status. Now, if you can remove status from your mind and do not seek it at all, then you accept what job you can, don't you? And then that job becomes interesting. I don't know if you follow—somebody disagrees with all this. Yes, sir.

Q: It's more complicated than that.

K: I know, it's much more complicated! [*laughter*] Because I'm married, I have children, I want more money, cars, a position. You know, all the responsibility of having a family in the modern world. It becomes terribly complicated. So how will you answer the problem each of us has? I may want a very simple job, I really don't care whether I'm a cook, a gardener, or a prime minister, which I'm not, thank God! I really don't care, because I'm not seeking status, so I'm only concerned with good functioning. Someone else may want a good position, be driven by ambition, always competing, being aggressive, and being aggressive he has his own problems, and so on. So, please listen to this, how will you answer this question so that the answer applies to every kind of human being who wants a job? And for every vacant job there are about three thousand people after it!

I was told the other day that somebody advertised for a cook, and BAs and MAs applied. So how will your answer to this question be one that will be acceptable to and true for everyone? Then it won't be complex, will it? We're going to find out—I haven't thought about this before, we're going to inquire into it together—whether there is an answer that will apply to every human being. Does one seek a job according to one's temperament? Depending on one's character, or on the demands of society—society wants there to be more engineers or scientists, or more artists—you may want to be an artist because you have a better position, are more respected, as in Russia, where you have special houses and special facilities.

Now, are you dependent on your temperament when seeking a job, that is, on your character? Please listen to this. We're inquiring, I'm not laying down the law, I'm not the Delphic oracle.

So am I seeking a job according to my temperament, which says, "I love that job"? And my temperament, my character is the outcome of my conditioning. So the job is decided on according to my conditioning and character. Or my conditioning expresses itself in peculiar idiosyncrasies—as an artist, a scientist, this or that. Shall I seek a job according to my idiosyncrasies, which means according to my conditioning? The conditioning is the result of the society I live in, and that society says, "Prestige, status is what is most important, not the function." And so my conditioning says, "I must get to the top of my profession for the prestige it has."

So being brought up in the culture in which I have lived, shall I follow the dictates of that culture, be dependent on temperament and idiosyncrasy, or what? Go on, what shall I do? So I ask myself, what is a human being to do who is very serious, living in this society with all its complexity—perhaps you see more of the complexity than I, but it is complex, so what shall a human being do? Knowing all this, knowing what is relationship, in which there is no image—we went into that—knowing that knowledge is necessary, having an insight into the whole process of thinking, what it means to lead a religious life, what it means to live religious meditation; knowing, observing all this, what shall he do? Just go and seek a job that he loves, a job dictated by his character, temperament, idiosyncrasy, conditioning? Or when he sees the whole picture, when things—you know, all the things we have discussed, talked about—are very clearly laid out, what will he do? Please look at it. What will he do?

Can I leave that question with you, or do you want the speaker to answer it? Look, what will you do? You, who have listened—we have discussed, gone into, the question of psychological revolution, and that is the only revolution, not violence. We discussed, went into together, shared together the whole question of relationship. We talked about knowledge, the necessity and importance of knowledge, and, at the same time, freedom from the known, and the two living, moving together. We have talked over religion, authority, love, and death, and a mind that is so marvelously clear that it lives in a different dimension, and so on. We've discussed all this. What shall I do, after hearing all this? What's my job after hearing all this? Well, what do you say? Do you want me to tell you? My job is what I am doing, to teach, to learn, to bring about a different human being—that is my job. If you have listened carefully right from the beginning, that will be your job. And if you don't love that job, don't do it.

# PART TWO

# 8 ⑨ BEING FREE OF PROBLEMS

To DELIBERATE IMPLIES not only to consider, weigh, think out together, but also to go into problems very deeply, slowly, carefully, knowing one's own prejudices, one's own crankiness, so that one listens not only to the speaker but also to the reactions, resolves, and idiocies one has—if you will forgive me for putting it that way. So that seriously, and not separately, not divisively, not you taking one side and the speaker the other, but together we observe what is going on in the world. Not only in this particular country but throughout the world: in economics and science, and in politics with the Socialists, the Liberals, and Conservatives. So this is not just a weekend gathering but something very serious—not churchy seriousness, but rather a seriousness that lasts not only for the time we spend together but also afterward when we go our separate ways.

Deliberation also implies seeing, deciding, and then acting. All that is implied in that one good word. So together, not merely intellectually, sentimentally or fantastically, let us take a serious look at what is happening to all of us.

We must also bear in mind in deliberating together that there is no outside help. The speaker is not trying to help, impress, convince, cajole, or pressure you. We can leave all that to the politicians, the newspapers, the television, and to the temples, mosques, and churches around the world. So we are together in this, without any pressure or persuasion on the speaker's part, or you on your side taking a view and then holding on to that. We are together investigating the extraordinary and dangerous problems that we are faced with. No one knows what is going to happen in the future; there is immense uncertainty, chaos, and the world is becoming more and more sinister.

So we are going to look first at the world, not my world or your world but the world that is confronting us, what is going on in the scientific field, in the buildup of armaments, with the politicians clinging to, and fighting for, their particular ideologies. If one may ask, how do you approach these problems? Not only one's own particular problem but the problems that challenge and require determined action in the scientific world, in biology, economics, the world of social inequality, social immorality? How do we approach this? As someone British? As a Frenchman? As a Hindu? As a Muslim and so on? If we approach it with a particular view, we are conditioned by a motive, known or unknown, and therefore our approach will be limited. This is obvious, isn't it? If the speaker is holding foolishly on to his India, then he will look at the world with all its complicated problems from a particular, narrow view. So his approach to all these problems will be partial, self-interested, always very petty, very limited.

That is clear. So one is asking, and please ask yourself, how will you approach these problems? Not a particular problem, whether it be yours, or your wife's, your husband's, and so on, but how do you approach a problem as such? Which means, How do you meet a challenge? Something that you have to face, answer, and act on.

What is a problem? According to the root meaning in the dictionary, it is something thrown at you, something that you have to face and answer. Not with a response dictated by time, circumstances, in a pragmatic or casual way, or with a certain sense of smugness, or with certain obvious conclusions. So how do you come to it? We are deliberating together; forget the speaker. Personality doesn't enter into this at all; you can brush that completely aside. So in what way do we face a problem? And why do we have so many problems? All our life from birth until death, we are beset, worn out by problems—worry, uncertainty, and perpetual conflict, struggle, pain, anxiety, all the rest of it. So shouldn't we together find out how to deal with them? That is the first question.

We know every one of us has a problem of one kind or another—of health, old age, or some incurable, terminal disease, or some psychotic problems, or some fantastic, illusory, cranky problems, which we call religious problems! So please, let's together find out why from the beginning of our life until we die, there is this constant challenge of problems. Can we go into this together? Not the speaker explaining, and you accepting or rejecting it, but debating, deliberating, weighing up together. As we have said, a problem is something thrown at you; it is a challenge, which you have to meet, apply your whole brain to, not just a nervous response.

As a child when you leave home, you feel homesick, and when you are at school you have to learn how to write and to read all those terrible books. And that becomes a problem, doesn't it? Right from childhood, when you go to school, college, university, and so on. And if you are a laborer, *that* becomes a problem. The whole of life becomes a problem. So our brains are conditioned from childhood to the resolution of problems. Again, I am not explaining this and you are just accepting it. We are together in the same boat. You may row faster, have more strength, more skill, others may be weaker, but we are in the same boat. So is that clear? That our brains from childhood are conditioned to problems; we live with problems. That is obvious, isn't it? The problem of sex, the problem of relationship, the problem of power, status, position, authority, and of dominating, obeying and disobeying, the whole movement of life.

So can we listen to, or hear, our own conditioning: that we are conditioned, trained, educated to live with problems? And with the resolution of one problem you create other problems, which the politicians do so remarkably well. And we are doing the same. So is it possible—we are deliberating together, please don't listen only to the speaker—is it possible first to have a brain free of problems and then tackle problems? Is it possible? Let us start by saying I don't know and you don't know.

So we are inquiring into that first. We have many very complicated issues in life. There is the whole personality, the whole activity of the brain, with so many feelings, sentiments, urges, attachments. And we never seem to resolve any of the issues but just to gradually wither away and die. So it becomes very important, doesn't it, to you and to all of us, to find out whether the brain, which has been trained to live with, participate in, be active with problems—please think this out with me—can have no problems at all and therefore tackle problems? Because it is only the free brain that can understand and resolve them. Not a brain that is itself crowded with problems. Scientists are crowded with them. Scientists with their theories and so forth are crowded with problems as human beings. They are first of all human beings and then scientists, right? So there is a constant movement or continuous chain of problems.

Now, how can we resolve this? Can you, we together, resolve this question? Which is very serious, because we are facing a very dangerous world. Politicians and ideologists are on different sides, and one side has an immense sense of power. And both sides are waiting. And we are caught in the middle of it. And there is also immense poverty in the world, poverty unknown to you in this country, immense poverty, degradation, corruption, and so on.

So we are asking ourselves whether our brains can be free to resolve problems. You have to answer that, not remain inert. So what will you do? Whatever you *do* will be another problem. You say, I will do this, I won't do that, I will believe this, I won't believe that, this is true, this is false, I pursue what I want. All that creates more problems, doesn't it? So again it behooves us first to find out whether our brains can be free of problems, so that we can then understand and resolve them.

Perhaps you have not thought about or gone into this question. You will say, "Give me time to think it over. Let me observe carefully, look, and then decide." If you allow time—which means, I will think about it, I will weigh the pros and cons, find where problems are unavoidable, where they are avoidable, and so on—if you take time over this, what happens? You tell me. What happens if I take time over some problem that needs to be resolved immediately, instantly? If it is not possible to resolve it instantly, won't other problems start to creep in? So will you solve the problem instantly? Solve this problem, the challenge: Your brain has been trained for so many years to live and move among problems that your brain is never free. Isn't that the very first problem?

Because we have got to face several complicated issues as we go along. Why we human beings, who have lived for thousands of years on this extraordinarily beautiful earth have changed psychologically, subjectively, very little. We are still barbarians in the real sense of that word. Why haven't we moved away from this set pattern after these countless years? That is a problem. Why is the world divided into nationalities, into religious activities; why have we been fighting each other, killing each other, the appalling things that occur in wars from the club to the atom bomb, why are we still going on like this? Why do we elect the politicians we do? Why are we so frightened of the future? We have many, many problems, right?

So it is important for each one of us to ask, What shall we do? What will you do? Of course, if you are obsessed by diet, or yoga, or some kind of fanciful, imaginative, cranky thing, then you are obviously lost. You are hooked on something. And you will never solve any of the problems. So what shall we do together, knowing that there is no outside help? Knowing you can attend all the meetings in the world, go to all the gurus in the world—and the speaker is not a guru—and, except perhaps physically, nobody can help you, neither your husband, your wife, your girlfriend, nor the priests or the scientists.

Can we put aside altogether the idea of wanting to be helped, wanting to be told, wanting to follow somebody, to believe in something? All that becomes irrelevant when you have got to deal with something *actual*. The *actual* is what we are: the multiple problems, the tears, the laughter, the agony, the anxiety, jealousy, hate, the psychological wounds.

So what shall we do together? We cannot live separately. Even the monks in their abbeys and monasteries in the Western world depend on each other. In the Asiatic world, especially in India, the monk wanders by himself all over the earth, all over India. And they have their problems. I don't know if you have ever followed a group of monks. Once the speaker was following a group of them in India, in the Himalayas, and they were chanting, reading their books, never hearing the song of the beautiful stream they passed by, never seeing the flowers, the extraordinary skyline of the snow-clad mountains twenty-five thousand feet high, never looking at all the beauty of the earth. They were just concerned with themselves and their little gods.

So please answer this question about yourself: whether your brain can be free, so that you can understand and dissolve problems. Can one see directly for oneself that one's brain is not free, is so conditioned, see that for oneself, not be told about it, not from reading something in a book, being convinced by someone else? Can we do that?

Are we aware that our brain is living with problems? Not as an observer looking through a microscope, whether rightly or wrongly, but be aware that our brains are so terribly conditioned to live with problems. Now suppose I am not aware of it, I have never even thought about it, I have never heard such a thing before. But now you have raised the question, Is it possible or not possible? And my brain being fairly active, not too dull, not hooked on something, my brain then begins to ask, Can it observe its own activity? Can the brain be aware of its own limitation and conditioning? Just as you observe yourself in a mirror when you shave, or make up your face—sorry! Can you in the same way observe your brain? Not as someone observing as an outsider, because the outsider is also the observed. There is no difference between the outsider and the insider. You don't say when you shave your chin that you are looking at your face from the outside; you are there in the mirror. You might have a difficult beard to shave, but you are there; your image is you. You don't say, "Well, I look different there from me." You are what you are.

So can the brain become aware of itself, its thoughts, its reactions, its way of living? Because that is the center of all our activity. And do we realize that? It is the center of all our nervous responses, all our reactions, all our conditionings, feelings, pleasures, pains, fears, anxieties, loneliness, despair, and the search for love, all the rest of it. It is there. When there is no understanding of that, what can I do? Anything I do will be meaningless. I wonder if you capture all this?

So are we aware of the activity of the brain? Why you think a particular thing, what your reactions are, why you are so cranky, psychopathic, why you cling to something, why there is this loneliness, sorrow, pain, grief, the anxiety and uncertainty. We are deliberating together, please. What shall I do if I am not aware? I know I am not. I am not aware of myself, myself being the brain, the thing that is restless, the thing that is always living in shallow valleys and deep valleys, that is always seeking self-interest. Whether it is seeking in the name of God, love, social reform, or seeking power, position, there is always this background. Are we aware of all this? If I am not, what shall I do? Help me! Sorry, that was a slip! [*laughs*] I am not asking for your help, let's talk it over.

We have sought help from everybody: from books, priests, psychologists, politicians, from every angle, every corner. And that help has been useless, because we are what we are now; we may have changed a little here and there, but actually we are what we are. In spite of all the help, in spite of all the leaders, the gurus, the ancient prophets, the ancient books! So could we put aside altogether the idea of seeking help? That doesn't mean you shouldn't be here and I shouldn't be here.

So is thought aware of itself thinking? This is not intellectual. Do you understand my question? Can your thought be aware of itself? If it cannot, then what will you do, or not do, to become completely aware of every movement of thought? Will you pray, ask somebody else? You can't do it by any of those ways. So can one remain quiet and watch? We mean by watch, to observe without a single movement of the word, the picture, the symbol, which is in essence thought. Can you observe first? Observe without a single activity of the past? Go on, come with me. Can you observe? Can I observe my pain, my physical pain, be aware of it? Not say, "I must rush to the doctor, take a pill," but just be aware of it. Psychologically be aware of it without any movement. Can you? And in the same way, observe the activity of the brain, not with lots of words and denials or assertions, but just observe. Have you ever observed your wife or husband, girlfriend or boyfriend, really observed them? Not with the images you have built about her or him; they are not observation, they are merely projection of the activities you have gradually built up, which becomes the image between you and her or you and him. So that is not actually observing.

What is the relationship—may I go on?—between observation and love? Is love merely .pleasure, merely a desire, a constructed thought? Is there division in that love, in the sense of "I love you and nobody else"? Or "I love you, but I am jealous of you." And is that love? We will go into that later. But we are asking now, When is there perception, observation? That can take place only when there is no motive, right? If I have a motive in that perception, in that observation, then that motive controls, shapes, molds the perception. So is there an observation without any motive? And motive is generally deeply hidden self-interest.

So we come to another very complicated issue: How far, how deep, is self-interest? To what extent can it be abandoned? Where do I put a stop to it? Is it possible to live in this modern world without any self-interest, without the whole spectrum of it? How deeply can the brain be free of it? Can the brain be absolutely free of it in the activities of daily life? Or in what degree? Or can one be without self-interest merely superficially?

This is a very complex problem. Because self-interest is the beginning of all corruption, the beginning of all divisive process, which is corruption. It is the origin of conflict. And how far, how deeply, or how shallowly can conflict come to an end? Not making it a problem, then we are lost again. Can conflict ever end between human beings, whether they are very close to each other or very far from each other; can conflict, struggle, the pain of it ever end? Come on, please. And what do we mean by conflict? Conflict is essentially a distortion; conflict in any form brings a distorted point of view. Conflict is essentially disorder. Are we together *deliberating* this, weighing it, considering it, with a view to act? The word means that. So can conflict end? So then the brain is free and can fly. Because the brain has immense capacity, but we are restricting it, narrowing it down with self-interest and conflict. So can conflict end?

Why is there this divisive element in us? You and I, we and they, and we are this and you are that—what is the origin of it? Is it the contrariness of desire? Is it the opposing elements of thought? Is it the ideal and the fact? The *should be* and *what is*? Is it that conflict begins when there is this dualistic process in all of us? Please, we are going together on the same path; we are in the same boat. Are we aware of this central fact that there is this dualistic force, the good and the bad, at work in all of us? This is an important question.

Is the good related to the bad? The speaker is putting a lot of eggs in one basket, a lot of things together, which are part of our life. We have a limited time, we must cram everything in! Are we aware of this central fact? Our morality is always balanced between the good and the bad. So one has to ask, Is the good related to the bad? Is the noble related to the ignoble, and so on? When one is rather cowardly and desires to be courageous, is that courage really courage, or is it partly born out of cowardice? So we are asking, What is the bad? And what is the good? If the good is related to the bad, then it is not good. When that which is beautiful is related to that which is ugly, then that beauty is born out of ugliness. Then it is not beautiful. I don't know if you are following this. Good born out of that which is not good is partial, and not being whole, it is not good.

So morality is not a balance of these two. I wonder if you see this? Can one be free of this duality, the dualistic process? This question, the good and the bad in conflict with each other, has been there for fifty thousand years or more. In the ancient cave paintings in France and other parts of the world, you see the good and the bad always fighting. And the outcome of that struggle is considered to be the highest morality. The good can never be related to the bad. Love cannot be related to hate, to anger, to jealousy. If it is so related, then it is not love; it is part of pleasure, desire, and so on.

So for God's sake, can some or all of us live on this earth without a single conflict? You can't answer this question, but let the seed of that question operate. Because if that seed is alive, not just the theory of it, then it has its own tremendous vitality, not your thinking about it and saying, "Well, I must understand what the devil he is talking about."

If one may suggest, let that seed grow. Say you have planted in the earth a seed of a peach tree, an oak, or whatever it is. You don't pull it up every day to see if it is growing, you leave it in the earth. So if the question has vitality, energy, then that very question begins to grow and act. You don't have to do anything; the thing itself is moving. Can we do that together? You are helping to plant a seed and I am digging the earth. It is work we are doing together. So the question has tremendous significance in itself, not the answer, not the result, but the question: Is it possible to live in this world, with all its complications, without a single shadow of conflict? You have planted it in your brain; let it remain there, see what happens.

So have you planted that seed? That means has each one of us listened to the question? Not only with the hearing of the ear, but listening to the actual fact of it. The fact that we have lived on this earth for countless or forty-five thousand years—and certainly not just four thousand years, as the fundamentalists like to think—and we are still living in conflict. So this is a very serious question, not only about the brutal conflict of war but about conflict between ourselves. Don't say, "I must understand what he means." He doesn't mean a thing. He means we are together. And is the seed, to live without any conflict, planted deep, in the deep valley of the brain, where there is soil, much richer soil than the soil of the earth? And from there it can grow, the answer, the decision, the action upon it.

# 9 🌀 THE LIMITATIONS OF
## TIME AND THOUGHT

---

THERE IS NO AUTHORITY in these dialogues between us. The speaker has unfortunately to sit on a platform, but that doesn't give him any authority. This is not a personality cult. And what he says is not something for you to think about and act on later. Here and now we are going together to explore and in so exploring to act.

We have talked recently about conflict. All the terrible things we are involved in: terrorism and the wars caused by division between different ideological, religious, and political beliefs. And nobody seems to care about the whole problem of the world. Each country with its own boundaries is battling economically with other countries. There is the threat of war and other terrible events. And we ought to consider all these matters.

But first of all did we see the marvelous clouds this morning? The beauty of them, the light of the extraordinary blue sky, the sense of glory? We ought to consider together what is beauty and what is love, what is time and thought. And if we have time we will also talk about fear.

So beauty, love, time and thought, and fear. The fear of

falling ill, of not being really well. We will go into that later. But first let us talk over the nature of beauty together. Please don't wait for the speaker to explain everything. This is a question for each one of us, like all the other questions we are going to look at together. What is beauty? And what is the relationship of beauty to thought and time and love? A beautiful cloud, a lovely sunset, the early morning when there is only one star in the sky and the trees are full with the sound, whisper, and movement of the leaves. And the earth itself, the enormous depth of the valleys, the power and outline against the blue sky of the great snow-capped mountains.

When you look at all that, and you look at your wife or your husband, the children running about this place, what does beauty mean to you? Does beauty depend on our own particular point of view? On our own sensitivity? Is beauty in the paintings confined to museums? In an ode of Keats? Or perhaps you read a sentence in a great work of literature, and that one sentence is enough to open all the doors. So for each one of us, what does beauty mean? Is it the face, the body, the sense of tenderness toward another, a sense of generosity, of giving, of great pleasure in seeing some marvelous painting?

Are you waiting for the speaker to tell you what beauty is? Or is beauty there when the self is not? You understand? When I am not worried about my own problems, my own misery, depression, and all the travail of life that is centered in me, which *is* the "me"? And when that "me" ceases to be, even if only for a split second, so that the brain is quiet without any sense of limitation, is there then beauty? And only then? Are we talking all this over, deliberating together? Or are we just agreeing with the speaker, saying to oneself, "Yes, that sounds good. That's the explanation I am looking for"—and according to that explanation and description, catching a glimpse of something and saying, "I will remember that"?

But then one asks, Does memory, the continuity of memory, the whole movement of memory, help in the apprehension of that which is beautiful? Or does remembrance have nothing whatever to do with it? And one also asks, *Is there* beauty in our life? The sense of generosity, the sense—not of forgiveness, there is nothing to forgive, but of great sensitivity? Belief, comparison, worry, and problems have nothing to do with beauty. It is that sense of quality that is the absence of the self, the "me," the persona, of all the background that is the "me"; it is in the absence of that, that the other is.

This may sound impossible, but is it? Are we talking about something extreme? Or it is the common lot of all of us that we go through great periods of suffering, agony, despair, depression, every kind of emotional upheaval, and also rare moments in our life when all that slips away from us, and we see something that is beyond all description? It does happen to all of us. And that becomes a memory. Then we pursue that memory. We want something more, continuing that which we have glimpsed. Then that memory becomes a block and destroys everything else.

We ought also to talk here about the very complex problem of time. Time as hope, time as the past, as all the events and happenings of our life. Time as the movement of memory, time as the longevity of one's life, time as living and dying on this earth. Time by the clock, the sharpness of a second in a quartz watch. Time as psychological becoming: "I am this but I will be that. I am unhappy, one day I will be happy. I will understand one day. There will be peace on earth sometime, but not now." So time is a very important factor in our life. Time as memory, time as evolving to something else, being surrounded in heaven by angels.

So time is an important factor and part of our life. And we think in terms of time. Time as what we have been, what is, and what we will be. I have been that, I am this now, but I will be something else in the future. This movement is the movement of experience, knowledge, memory, the constant movement between the past, the present, and the future. This is very important in our life. Time creates a lot of problems. One is looking forward to something, a holiday in Spain or the lovely Sicily, and so on.

Has this movement a stop? We are taking counsel together. Has this everlasting movement, which seems to extend from the beginning of one's life till one dies, ever a stop? Please, we are putting this question for you. Let the question answer, not what you answer. Do you understand that? The question is very important. The question is, Does time, this movement, this cycle in which we have all of us been caught endlessly for the countless years we have lived on this earth, can this ever end? Or is a human being eternally caught in it? This is not science fiction or a theory about time or some fantastic "otherness"; we are putting a very simple and direct question to each other. The question is important because only then can something totally new take place.

So can time ever stop? Time as old age, and in old age one becomes slightly gaga. Senility takes place. This is rather an interesting subject! Who is senile? Is it only the young, the young up to thirty or forty who are not senile, and all the rest of us are? Or are only elderly people senile? What is senility?

When you go to a church and the cardinals are performing, it is a marvelous, a beautiful sight, so carefully worked out, so precise, so dignified, with marvelous robes and color. But there is of course repetition in that ritual. And is repetition the indication of senility? And is that found only in the old? There is repetition of the same habit, the same way of thinking, perpetually going to the office and the factory. And repetition of the same relationship with each other, sexually, or getting so used to each other that there is never any sense of feeling that you are entirely alone on this earth. Our brain is caught in repetition. Repetition has its own security, its own safety, offering protection, but when in the psychological sphere you keep on remembering and acting in the same old way, that is naturally a form of senility, isn't it? Don't, please, agree. It is not a matter of agreeing or disagreeing. One wishes we could rid ourselves of those two words *agreeing* and *disagreeing*. It is a question of *seeing* what is actually taking place in us, and observing the habits we have formed over many years, the conclusions that we have, politically, religiously, and so on. By *conclusion* meaning this is what I have understood, I stick by it, and so on. Is that not a form of senility, and one not confined to the old?

So we are talking about time. The past going through the present, modifying and continuing. The past has taken deep roots and moves in the present through challenges, circumstances, pressures, and so on, but it is still the past. And the future is the past, modified. So the future is now, isn't it? The present is what we have been and what we are. That is a fact. And that past gets molded, shaped, pressured, undergoes every kind of travail, anxiety, and so on, but continues in a modified form in a variety of ways, and that becomes the future. So the future is now. Are we together in this, or do we need further explanation?

Is the whole movement of the past, the present, and the future contained in the now? Because that is what we are. And that is the whole movement of time. And we are asking, Will that movement ever stop? Otherwise we are bound to the everlasting time-binding quality of this movement of the past, present, and future. And we escape from that question by talking about heaven, hell, the future, which is away from all this. So as you are now sitting there we are saying that all time is contained in the now, which is the past, modifying itself in the present and the future. Can this cycle, this movement that is the now, stop for a minute, for a second?

Then one asks, What is timelessness? Setting aside all theories, all beliefs about time, the heavens have their own order and sense of timelessness, but all that has nothing to do with our actual daily, boring, lonely, despairing, and occasionally joyous lives. So is there an end to time?

And what is the relationship of time to thought? Please ask yourself these questions. And the relationship of time and thought to fear? And their relationship to love? This is what we are concerned with.

So what is thought, which is so important, which is so deeply embedded in the recesses of our brain? What is the role of thought, thinking, in our life? Please ask this question of yourself. All this has nothing to do with religions, with all that circus with the gurus, with spiritual authority. Just think of those two words together: spiritual authority! It seems such an abomination, anathema, to put the two together.

All one's life and action are based on thought. And you may say emotions are not thought. Now, is that so? We are so gullible, we accept everything so easily. Somebody like the speaker says something and you say yes or no. But that is not your own thinking, not your own clear, objective, nonpersonal observation of everything. We are full of other people's knowledge, but we don't know how our own brain works. We go spiritual window-shopping, collecting a bit here, then off to somewhere else for a bit more. It sounds funny, doesn't it? We are always collecting like a magpie or a pack rat, and we don't know anything about our own capacity, a capacity that is not based on experience, that has nothing to do with knowledge.

So what is thinking? You are sitting there and the speaker is on this unfortunate platform, and we are both thinking. What does that thinking mean? He says something, a question is put to you, and the brain starts to become active; it is being challenged, driven, pushed, pressured, and then it wakes up and says yes or no. And so we go on. We never dig into ourselves, which means we depend on so many things, so many books, professors, gurus, or leaders. So here we are without a leader, without help, without any kind of circumstantial, pragmatic sustenance. You have to find out what is thinking, what is the origin of all thought, not just a particular thought. Thought obviously has a cause. And what has a cause can always be overcome. So what is the cause of thinking? If one understands the cause, then one can put the cause aside.

If one can discover the cause, the raison d'être, the root of it, it is possible to uproot it and let it wither away and die. Or it is not possible, because one has not discovered the root for oneself. If one can discover the cause, the effect has no meaning, then the cause will die. That is what we are going to find out together: What is the cause of thought, thought being associated with remembrance, with memory, the images that thought has put together? Is it experience? Is it experience that gives rise to knowledge? And the knowledge is stored in the brain as memory and that memory reacts as thinking? Is all thinking based on that? Is it as simple as that? Thinking is based on familiarity, on memories. If you had no memory, you wouldn't think, right? Let's be very simple.

So is thinking based on experience, knowledge, memory? Thinking is always based on knowledge. The more knowledge you have, the more you think. Science is adding more and more every day. First there was a simple club, then there was archery, then the gun, and then ultimately the atom bomb. All that is based on accumulated knowledge. Step by step, or with a sudden jump, but still within the field of knowledge. So however simple this may sound, thinking is essentially based on experience, knowledge, memory. We are asking, Can that thinking stop? Otherwise we are caught in this. Can there be a state without a single memory, a single thought?

And the relationship between man and woman, the relationship between husband, wife, children, girlfriend and boyfriend, and so on, the closeness, the feeling for each other—is that based on thought? The question itself is important, not the answer. So there is relationship and thought and time. I am married to you, for various reasons: sexual attraction, dependence, companionship, and all the rest of it. And as we live with each other for a day, or for ten or fifteen or a hundred years, we get used to each other, and have built up memories, images about each other. This is obvious, isn't it? And those memories, those images are the realities, not the woman or the man or the children. The reality is the image that I have built about her, and the image she has built about me. These images are functional realities, but they are not actual relationship.

So thought is the basis of our life, whether working in a business, a mine, or a laboratory. All the things that the priests have put together—the rituals, the beliefs, the wafers—and all the things that are in the temples and mosques are all put together by thought. And thought, being based on knowledge, is therefore everlastingly limited, partial. There is no complete thought, right?

So there is recognition of the fact that thought is completely limited. Your worship, your prayer, your belonging to this guru or to that guru—for God's sake, all that is so terribly trivial. Don't get angry, please, with me. If thought is limited, and it obviously is, you may think of the unlimited, but it is still limited. You may think of the eternal, but that is still put together by thought. And we are saying, Can that thought, time, come to an end? Probably you have never asked this question, and so you can't answer it, because you haven't delved into yourselves deeply, examined, looked, observed, which is different from analysis, just observing the deep layers of one's own life and brain.

From that we should move and inquire, What is fear? Is fear related to time and thought? What is fear? Fear of being ill. We have all been ill at one time or another. The earth is crowded with doctors and pills. What is the value or significance of being ill, of which you are so frightened? Has it any meaning at all? When fear interferes with illness, do you learn anything at all? Or can one look at that illness quite objectively, not immediately identify oneself with the pain and then battle with it, wanting to be healthy and so on?

If one allows illness to be, not to the extreme of terminal illness, it has a great significance, it indicates a great deal, it opens the door to many things. But when there is fear, all the doors are shut tight. So we are now also inquiring, What is fear? Fear of losing pleasure, fear of tomorrow, fear of darkness, fear of one's husband or wife, fear of your guru—of course fear of your guru, otherwise you wouldn't follow him, out of fear of not getting his peculiar enlightenment! Think of it: a guru having enlightenment! Fear of so many things: one's neighbor, war, terrorists, and all the things that the priests have put together for two thousand years in Christianity, and all the extraordinary traditions that ancient India has put together for three to five thousand years.

So there is the fear of heaven and hell, and fear of the most trivial things of our life. Let us look together at the cause of fear. As we said, if you can discover the cause for yourself, then you can deal with the cause. If you observe it very carefully, then that very cause comes to an end. You don't have to do anything about it, just observe the cause as you observe something external, just as you heard the rain a few minutes ago; you hear it and if you hear it quietly it tells you something, it has its own music.

What is the cause of fear? There is fear of illness, fear of death, fear of a hundred little things, fear that inhibits freedom. As long as there is any particle of fear of anything, there is no freedom. First we must deal with the psychological fears, not the external fears—they come later. If psychological fears are ended completely, then you will deal with physical fears entirely differently, not the other way around. But we want to be fearless outwardly, and therefore we divide ourselves into countries, beliefs, dogmas, and all that childish business. What is needed is to see the root of inward, psychological fear, not as a separate person with "my" fears, but seeing the phenomenon of fear as a whole, because every human being goes through fear. Even the gurus, even the priests, even the highest authority in Christendom, they all have fears. All over the world every human being has the fear of death, of lacking love, and, oh, dozens and dozens of fears. And because we have fears we are never free, so it behooves us to examine very closely, though not analytically, because then you separate the analyzer and the analyzed and conflict begins.

So fear, like pain, anxiety, sorrow, uncertainty, the demand for power, position, prestige, is common to all of us; every human being has this seed of fear. We are not talking about a particular fear, because when one grasps the root, the whole content of fear, then you can deal with the particular. So what is the root of fear? Please don't wait for the speaker to explain. The root of it, which will be found in us, not in heaven, or in the priests—is it time? Is it thought? Is it some unknown factor that has been a curse for human beings for some two million years? That long evolution has not solved this problem; we have escaped from it, worshiping gods, following somebody, all that business. So can we, deliberating together, find out the cause and end it? End it now, not the day after tomorrow. If you end it now, you will be an amazingly free human being. Then you are really free. And that freedom alone can open the door to truth.

So we are asking, What is the root of it? Is it thought? Is it time? Don't please accept a thing that the speaker says, and don't copy his words, but go into it. You need passion to have the tremendous energy to discover anything, not just accepting another's words and handing over yourself to somebody. This is a very serious question, nothing to do with all that immature stuff. So are thought and time responsible? Or are time and thought one, not separate? Is that the root of it? It is the root of it, isn't it? If one is afraid of death, of that ending taking place in the future, then one is frightened by the thought of the unknown. So is thinking whose root is time the root of fear? Of course. It is obvious if one points it out. If we do not think of death and there is no time, there is no fear of death.

Therefore the question arises, Can thought-time stop? Only then is there the end to fear. But one has to see it for oneself, not take it from another, not be a beggar. Nobody is giving or taking here. Nobody is stretching his hand out to you to make you move. You have to have the energy, and that energy has its own capacity. So the speaker is saying—which you don't have to accept or reject, just listen to him—that fear can end psychologically completely, wholly, when there is no thinking and time. That inquiry itself, to find out the cause of fear, and on finding it out for oneself, holding that cause, staying with it, that very staying has its own energy. But if you run away, you are playing a game with yourself. So is it possible to end fear now, psychologically and so completely that you are a free human being?

We will talk about other things, like pleasure, sorrow, meditation, religion, and so on. But if fear doesn't come completely to an end, these other things are meaningless. You may sit and meditate, wear special robes, follow some person—all of that has no meaning. What has meaning is the ending of fear. And when you discover the cause, which is thought and time, remain with it, hold it, stay with it, don't let it escape from your hands. Then the very observation of that is the ending of psychological fear, an ending in which there is no attachment to anything.

# 10 ✿ QUESTIONS AND ANSWERS 1

M AY I MOST RESPECTFULLY and seriously ask you why
you are here? Is it out of curiosity, with nothing better to do? I am asking this respectfully, not impu-
dently. Are we here to be stimulated, to be challenged, to indulge
in merely intellectual flirtation—that is a good word!—or do we
want romantically, sentimentally, some kind of help from another? If one asked oneself these questions, what would one answer? Of course, you might also ask the speaker why he is talking.
Is it a habit? Is it because he needs an audience to feel happy, ful-
filled? Such questions must also be put to the speaker, who has
been going to various continents and talking for the last sixty or
seventy years. So has it become a habit? He has tested this by
keeping quiet for more than a year to examine very carefully
whether he depends on others to fulfill, to be, to become, to feel
famous, all that nonsense. So in return, he is asking you, respectfully, why you are here.

So is it because we have nothing better to do, or is it that we
really, deeply, want to understand ourselves? He is only acting as
a mirror in which, without being depressed or elated, we can see
ourselves as we are. In that mirror, is every feature clear, sharp,

without any distortion? And if the mirror is clear, and you see yourself exactly as you are, then the mirror is not important. You can break it without worrying about bad luck! And can you answer the question—a rather serious one—why we behave as we do: why we think in a certain pattern; why we follow somebody, the crazier the better; why we store up all the things that others have said; why there is nothing in ourselves that is original. So can we discover the deep-rooted seed of what we are, not only the cultural, traditional, religious seed, all the outgrowth of that, but go very deeply into oneself to find out the origin of all things? Not the cells, the genes, that one has inherited, but something far beyond all that.

Shall we go into that a little bit? What is the origin, not the biological and evolutionary process, but the origin of all things? This raises the question, What is creation? Who created all this, the marvelous universe, everything living in and out of it? What is the origin of all that? Do you want to go into this?

AUDIENCE: Yes.

KRISHNAMURTI: Are you sure? Why? As an amusement? As a form of entertainment, something novel? I am afraid it is not anything like that.

Our brains have extraordinary capacity, a capacity going beyond all ordinary things. Look at the tremendous advances in the technological world, what they have done, are doing, are going to do. The computer is going to take over increasingly all our activities, more or less, except sex, and probably it won't be able to look at the stars of an evening. It may bring about a new industry, a new way of living. There is tremendous competition between America and Japan in this area. And we will all be slaves to the new god of the computer. So the brain has this extraordinary capacity, but it has been restricted, narrowed down by our education, by our self-interest. The brain, which has evolved for millions of years, has become what it is now—old, tired, with a lot of trouble, conflict, and misery. That brain, which is the center of all our existence, all our being, which is the future and the past, that brain wants to find out what is beyond all this, what is the origin, the source, the beginning.

Can it ever find out? Can it ever find out what is the source of life, the beginning of all creation, of all things, not only of ourselves but of the tiger, the marvelous trees? Have you ever been very close to a tiger in the wild? The speaker was once very close, almost touching it. And who brought about this inexhaustible nature, the rivers, the mountains, the trees, the lawns, the groves, the orchards, and us? How will you find out? Please ask this question of yourselves. How will ordinary human beings like us find out something sought by scientists, biologists, and the archaeologists discovering new cities? How will we find out? By following somebody? By making some guru inexhaustibly rich? How will you go into this? That is my question to you. Who will answer it? Are you waiting for the speaker to answer it? Or will you invent a new God who will say he created it? Such invention, such imagination, is still the product of the brain.

So how will you find out? May I leave you with that question? What will you give to it to find out—give in the sense of your energy, your capacity, your enthusiasm, your passion, all the time you have? Or will you just say, "Oh, I am too busy right now, I will think about it tomorrow" or "That is a question for the older not for the younger generation"? So how much energy will you give to it?

QUESTIONER: At times we have had mystical and spiritual experiences. Unless we know reality, how can we know that they are not illusions?

KRISHNAMURTI: How do you answer such a question? If it was put to you, how do you approach it, what is your reaction? How do you come so close to it that the question itself unfolds and begins to evolve? To find an answer is fairly easy, but to delve into the question, to see all its complications, is like having the map of the world in front of you, seeing all the countries, the capitals, villages, hamlets, rivers, the ocean, the hills, the mountains, the whole of it. How do you look at this question? Not come up with the answer. Perhaps the answer to the question may lie in the question.

The questioner says that at times we have had mystical and spiritual experiences. What is an experience? And who experiences? I may have had or be having some kind of mystical experience. Before I use the words *mystical* or *experience*, what do I mean by *experience*? Does experience involve recognition? Does it involve a sense of something coming to me from heaven or somewhere, of something or other that I call *mystical*, which is not daily experience but something totally outside that? And I call that mystical or spiritual. I would like, if I may, to stick to the two words *spiritual* and *experience*.

Is there an experience without an experiencer? Are we exploring the question together, or are you waiting for the speaker to explore it? Are we walking together, step by step? Then we are friends talking over this problem. Suppose I have had a spiritual experience. What do I mean by those two words? Is an experience something that is new, or something that I have had in the past but which is now renewed, or something that is happening to the experiencer? And if the experiencer is experiencing, and that experiencing is a form of recognition, that is, the remembrance of and identification with that which I call experience, there must in that be the feeling that I have already known it, otherwise I couldn't recognize it. That is fairly simple, isn't it?

As long as there is an experiencer experiencing, then it is something that is happening to the experiencer, something separate, something that is not ordinary, that is not a daily, boring, habitual experience that one has, right? So as long as the experiencer is there, whatever the experience—call it mundane, spiritual, holy, sacred, release of energy, and all that mostly nonsensical stuff that goes on—what is most important in this process is the experiencer. He is gathering. So when there is an experiencer, it gets more and more subliminally egotistic, more and more "I know a great deal that you don't know. I have had a marvelous spiritual experience, I am illumined. You, poor chap, are not, so come along with me. Give me all your money and you will be quite safe." That is the game they are playing, I assure you—"Surrender yourself. Put on these beads that I give you."—all that rather silly game.

So what does *spiritual* mean? Something holy? Something unexpected? Something totally out of the ordinary? Why do we want something totally different from our daily life? Please answer this question. Because we are bored with our daily life—the habits, the loneliness, the despair, the attachments, power, and all the rest of it? We want to avoid all that and invoke heaven, which is called being spiritual. We can deceive ourselves enormously, incredibly. Christianity is based on belief and faith. Sorry, I am not trying to hurt anybody, just pointing this out. This has been so for two thousand years. And cross the ocean to India, and belief and faith have been there for three or five thousand years. The same process of selling God. Why do we have to believe all this? Because we are frightened? Because we want to know the unknown and so on?

So what is illusion? And what is reality? The questioner asks, Unless we know reality, how can we know that they are not illusions? So we have to examine what is reality. What is reality? The real, the actual, is that you and the speaker are sitting here now, at twelve o'clock. That is actual. There is a wind, and I hope it won't rain. And the actual is nature, the birds, the rivers, the waters, and so on. And the questioner says, Unless I know reality, I can't know what an illusion is, right? So what is real in ourselves? Is there anything real, actual, in us? Or is it all a movement, change? The other day in Switzerland when we put an end to the Saanen gatherings, some people came up to the speaker and said, "We are so sad it has been closed." And the speaker said, "If you are sad, it is about time we closed it." Very few of us want fundamental change.

And the questioner says, If I knew reality, I'd know what illusion is. So we should look at the word *illusion*. What is illusion? In the dictionary the word is defined as something you play with: *ludere*. Something you invent and enjoy: I am God, I am whoever it is, Napoleon, or I am a great man. You play with something that is not actual. But when one has pain, despair, a sense of tremendous, unaccountable loneliness, that is actual, specific. And we create an illusion that somebody is going to help us, somebody is going to give us fulfillment, take away our loneliness. That is all illusion. The actual fact is that one is desperately lonely.

So it is fairly simple to see for oneself, if one wants to, what an illusion is, what reality is, and why there is this craze for experience. We have had sexual experience, thousands of experiences. Walking from here across the field you see the birds, the house-martins, and so on; that is an experience, but you don't call that spiritual. I see you sitting there; it is a challenge, something moving. So what is important in all this is why the experiencer invents. You see my point? Why has the experiencer become so important? Is there a time when the experiencer is not?

That is the real question, not what is reality, what is illusion, what is experience, and all the rest of it, but is there a period, a length of time, a space, when the experiencer, the observer, and so on, is not? Then you don't want experiences. There is nothing. *Nothing* is the right word. The word *nothing*—sorry, I am not a dictionary—means "not a thing." Not a thing put together by thought, you understand? Where there is nothing, not a thing put together by thought, there is the end of time and thought. That is when there is no experiencer at all. That is the real.

Q: Is illness due simply to degeneration or abuse of the body, or does it have some other significance?

K: We have all been ill at some time or other in our lives, or have had an accident and broken a bone. Has it any benefit? Does it make us understand deeply why we become ill, and what health is?

We have all been ill, and we don't like to put up with it for a bit, but immediately go to a doctor for pills. We never stay with it a little—not too long, of course—to see what pain implies, how we respond to it. I know how you respond to pleasure, that is fairly simple. But how do you respond to pain, not only physical pain but getting hurt psychologically? Psychological hurt is a form of illness, isn't it? If I get hurt because you are rude to me and say, "You are a silly ass," that is a form of illness. But when I get hurt physically, there is a doctor to go to, there is someone who can do something about it. I want to avoid psychological pain, just as I want to avoid, run away from, physical pain. So we never stay with being hurt and see what it is like.

Far more important than physical pain is psychological hurt, the feeling of deep agony inside. That is a great illness to which we don't pay much attention. Nobody can heal that inward pain for you. No pill, no guru, no book, no gods, no ritual will stop that pain. But if you don't run away from it, and stay really deeply with it, it has immense significance. Then you penetrate into something that goes beyond all self, all self-interest. The physical pain can then be dealt with—you go to a doctor, put up with it, and it becomes secondary.

So if you go into it for yourself, you will find that illness and psychological hurt have some significance. It depends on you— how you face life, how you look upon it, in what manner you receive it, in what way you react to it, how you respond to all the things that you are faced with in daily life, not just on Sunday mornings. So if one observes oneself closely as one observes a lovely tree, or a pigeon in flight, it is extraordinary what it reveals.

Q: What is my responsibility toward the present world crisis?

K: What is my responsibility toward the present world crisis? Who are you putting this question to? What is my responsibility, your responsibility? Why do we use the word *responsibility*? To be responsible. To be responsible for keeping your body clean. You are responsible for your children. The professors, the teachers, the educators are responsible for educating children. Why do we use that word *responsible*? You understand my question? If you eliminated the word *responsibility* because that word implies you and responsibility, would you put that question? It is my duty to kill for my country. It is my duty as a Russian or American or British citizen to fight for my country and God and all the rest of it. If we could remove the words *duty* and *responsibility* altogether from our brain, how would you answer this question? If you drop those words, what happens? That is a very interesting question. What takes place without this duality that is implied in responsibility? Are we together a little bit? The word *responsibility* implies I am responsible for you, for my children, for my wife, for my boss, for my job, and so on. I am responsible for presenting God to you. [*drops the paper with the list of questions*] Banish that word from your whole being, just like dropping this paper! Then what takes place? Have you done it? No, you haven't. You see, you hear something, but you don't act on it. I am not responsible for Brockwood. I, the speaker, don't feel that way. I am not responsible for telling you anything. But if that word is not, which means there is no I and my responsibility for you, there is only you and I, then what takes place?

Has love a responsibility? If love has no responsibility, then what takes place? If love is not attachment, which is implied in responsibility, then what takes place? Please, if I may respectfully point out, don't say anything that you have not lived, worked on to find out. If I love you, if the speaker loves you, and the words *responsibility, duty, attachment,* and so on are not, then what is our relationship? Go on, think it out. The speaker is not going to answer that question. It is really a very serious question.

So all this implies, Do we love anything? Love, meaning something that is not dualistic: "*I* love *you.*" Well, I have answered the question. No, *I* have not answered, the question has been answered, has evolved.

Q: Does asking for guidance necessarily prevent understanding? Cannot seeking help be a means of discovery of ourselves? If not, what is the sense of listening to you, K?

K: What is the sense of listening to K? There is no sense. If you are really truthful, you are not listening to him; you are listening to see where you agree or disagree. In the process of listening, you are translating what he says to your convenience, to your conditioning. But when you are really listening, you are listening not to K but to yourself. K is not talking about something extraordinary. There is something extraordinary far beyond all this, but he is not talking about that now. You are listening to yourself, right? As we said earlier, you are seeing yourself in the mirror. And you can distort the mirror, or say, "I don't like the mirror, I don't like what I see" and break it, but you are still what you are.

So you are not listening to K. You are not trying to understand what K is saying. You are actually listening to yourself. If you are listening to yourself for the first time, that is the greatest thing that can happen. But if you are listening to K, then there are just a lot of words, a lot of reactions, and so on. That is so utterly, if one may respectfully point out, meaningless, unnecessary. You have listened to so many things, to preachers, books, poems, you have listened to the voice of your wife or husband, or you just casually listen. But if you give all your attention to listening, hearing not only with the ear but hearing much more deeply, then you will listen to everything. You will listen to what K has to say, and either you live with it, and it is real, true, actual, or it is something verbal, intellectual, and therefore has very little meaning in one's life.

And the questioner asks whether seeking and asking for guidance necessarily prevents understanding? Understanding of what? Chemistry, mathematics, some philosophical concept? What do we mean by understanding? Please, I am not being rude, just asking. What do we mean by the word *understanding*? I understand French because I know some French. So that is intellectual, verbal communication. That is one form of understanding. We use a common language; you speak English and the speaker speaks English, and there is verbal communication, if we refer to the same thing and do not give words different meanings.

So what do we mean by *understanding*? A verbal communication? Intellectual comprehension of a concept, of an idea? Or does understanding mean actually listening to what another is saying, not trying to interpret, not trying to change it, not trying to modify it, actually listening to what he says, not only intellectually but with great attention, with all your being? Then it is not merely intellectual, emotional, or sentimental, all that stuff, but you are entirely present. Then there is not only verbal communication but also nonverbal communication.

And the questioner asks, Does guidance necessarily prevent understanding. Why do I want guidance? About what? You tell me, those of you who follow these gurus and all the rest of it, the churches and temples and mosques, what do you mean by guidance? Why does one want guidance from a fellow human being in a different kind of robe, with or without a beard, especially from Asia, including India? Are you being guided now? Be simple. Are you being guided now? Or are we together investigating, exploring, communicating, with you saying, "I don't understand what you are saying," and I say, "I'll explain it," and then you explain something to me and I say, "Yes." We are moving together, there is no guidance.

We have had guidance galore: Every newspaper, every magazine, every preacher, every priest throughout the world is guiding us, telling us what to do, what not to do, think this, don't think that, surrender yourself, don't listen to him, he is a reactionary, listen to me—you follow? We are being guided, shaped, molded, all the time, consciously or unconsciously. Here we are not guiding anybody, we are like two friends talking things over together. That is totally different. And guidance prevents understanding, in the deeper sense of that word, because if you are guiding me all the time, do this, don't do that, I can't understand myself first, I am not looking at myself, I am listening to what *you* have said. That means you become the authority, and I become your slave, either a psychological slave or some other kind of slave. These gurus' places, their ashrams, become concentration camps. They tell you what to do, how to salute, all that tommyrot. I am not condemning, it is so.

Why can't we be simple? See things as they are. Look at, face things as they actually are, instead of all this labyrinth and maze? Why do we have to go through all this? Except going to a doctor, that is a different matter. Psychologically is what we are talking about. Why can't we be very simple and look at things as they are? Is our brain so incapacitated, so cunning, so desperately devious that it cannot see things, what is in front of our nose or eyes? If you are very simple psychologically, that very simplicity has immense subtlety, much more subtlety than all the cunning of the brain. But we are never simple. If it is raining, it is raining. If I am lonely—the speaker is not—one is lonely, that is a fact. Why all the circus around it?

Q: Could you please explain what is total seeing? Is it an extension of our normal brain function? Or is something totally different implied?

K: To be very simple: Do we see anything entirely? Leaving aside trees and nature, all that, does one see one's wife or husband—actually see, not imagine, through all the images, but simply see? If I see partially, because I have so much prejudice, so much fear, so much anxiety, I never see the person entirely. To see someone or something holistically—if I may use that word—completely, wholly, means that in that seeing there is no contradiction, it is so. There is no contradiction in seeing what is actually going on. Say that I am angry, impatient, exhausted. I can see that simply. But the moment I think, "Oh, I shouldn't be angry, but I am like this, exhausted, exasperated, because, et cetera," and bring in excuses, I cannot see totally.

Can I see myself wholly as I am? Again, can I see the whole map? Say a map is put in front of each one of us, a map of the world, with various colors, various flags, various prime ministers, various presidents. There it is in front of me, in front of you. Can I look at the whole of the map? It is not possible to look at the whole map if my attention is focused on Britain or on Russia, directed to one place. So this direction of attention to one place, to self-interest, prevents the holistic outlook, the seeing of the whole thing. It is simple: If I am stuck or my roots are in this one particular corner of the earth, I cannot possibly see the whole thing. If I am always thinking about India, what is happening there, what makes me an Indian, why I am poor, why I am this or that, how I rely on some particular god or something or other, I am stuck there, I can't see the whole picture. It is as simple as that. And naturally when I see the truth of that, I say what nonsense the previous view was.

But there is much more to seeing than that. Observing without any words, without any interference of thought, just seeing. First of all visually, then inwardly seeing everything as it is. And from that seeing, one can go much further. Then one asks, What is insight? Seeing something to be absolutely true and acting instantly. I won't go into all that now. It requires investigation or observing, but without an analyzer of what one is. And from there you can move infinitely, boundlessly. Then there is no beginning or end.

# II ✿ QUESTIONS AND ANSWERS 2

WE ARE SO EASILY INFLUENCED, not only by television, books, newspapers, and magazines but also by past traditions. It may be the tradition of five thousand years or the brief tradition of a single day or afternoon going for a drive or walking in the woods, and all these influence us. So there is not only the genetic, hereditary process in each human being, but everything that exists seems to be engaged in a process of mutual influence—the air, pollution, the beauty of the earth, everything around us. We tell each other what to do, what to think; we put pressure on each other through beauty, through a lovely poem or a personal relationship. There seems to be a constant process of being molded, shaped, formed. And we proceed for the whole of our life on that narrow way, and it seems to be our way of existence. And one wonders if it is at all possible to be totally free of influence, to find the origin, the beginning of all things, which must have no cause or effect. . . .

So is that possible? We are talking over this together. The speaker is not trying to influence you, or you to influence the speaker. We are two friends talking, not of spiritual matters and that kind of stuff, but of ordinary matters, walking along a path that goes through the woods, aware of the dappled light, and the beauty of the trees and the earth. And is it ever possible, we are asking each other, to be free of all influence? Which means the past, which we are; that past has a tremendous influence on us, the age-old tradition of the so-called religious books, the ancient epics, whether the *Iliad* or the Hindu texts.

So let us ask whether it is possible to be free of all this and to be something totally original. Not the repetition of guru and disciple, the follower and the followed, with their peculiar garb and that business. Is it possible? Please give your attention to this. What do you think? Is it possible or impossible? If it is impossible or incredibly difficult, we choose the easiest way, follow the old pattern, only with a different set of leaders, teachers, gurus— and so-called enlightened birds! Is it possible to be something totally original? Or are we doomed to remain forever in this state of being impressed, shaped, molded, and conditioned?

What would you do if it were possible? How would you set about it? In what way would you approach this question? Perhaps that may be the real, the most important question. Because we are so gullible, we invent so many reasons for following, being led, surrendering oneself to something that seems so convincing, satisfying, handing over all "responsibility" to another. This has been our lot. And knowing all this, how would one come to see what actually is, and see what one can do? Not just talk about it.

Isn't it necessary to have a great deal of doubt, and a certain quality of skepticism, not only about others but about oneself? About one's desires, convictions, beliefs, faith, and definite, directive purposes? Can we question, doubt all that, and see how far that doubt, how far the sense of asking, demanding, inquiring can go? Could we do this together? Not leading each other with our convictions, but inquiring together.

Knowing that we need doubt and skepticism, which are very energizing and cleansing, will you go into this? Doubt one's own experiences, one's own attitudes, prejudices, agreement and disagreement, all that? Doubt is like having a dog on a leash: Sometimes at the right place you must let the dog run free, jump, otherwise the dog becomes rather dull.

Skepticism also has its right place, its own quality of rightness. "Oh, I won't doubt that, because I belong to that, but I will doubt everything else." We used to have a great many friends at one time, including Communists, and they would always go so far and no further, like the Catholics, the Protestants, the Hindus, the Buddhist monks. Beyond that, they would say, is mystery, to go beyond that is impossible.

So doubt must be kept on a leash, but also be allowed to run. Can we do that together? Doubt your gods, your gurus, your experiences, and doubt the whole background of human experience, endeavor, and conclusions, the whole bundle of it, and begin to inquire into that bundle? And see how far you can go in your daily life with doubt, inquiry, not theoretically but actually and passionately.

Now, how far is knowledge essential? How deep must it go? Not only knowledge of books and what others have said, but knowledge about ourselves. Knowledge is always limited, isn't it? You can see what scientific knowledge is achieving. Little by little, more and more is added to it. What is added to is naturally always limited. If I am adding something to knowledge all the time, knowledge is always limited, because there is always more to add.

But knowledge is the background that is guiding us, shaping us, telling us what to do. Or do you have intuition? That is a favorite word, but one that is also rather dangerous because intuition may be a sublimated wish or desire. So what place has knowledge in daily life? You have to have knowledge to write a letter, to speak English or a foreign language. You have to have knowledge to do business, when you telephone, drive a car.

Knowledge also acts in relationship. One recognizes one's

wife, one's husband, a friend, and such recognition is part of knowledge. But what place has knowledge in relationship? What place has knowledge between you and another? I know my wife, father, mother, husband. When we say "I know you," what place has that knowledge in daily life between man and woman, between wife and husband? Answer, please, what place does your knowing her have in your relationship? Is knowledge the impediment to relationship?

If I say to myself, "I know my wife," what do I mean by that? Past sexual experience, my irritation with her, her anger with me, or her saying how nice I am. All that builds up an image about each other. This is a fact, isn't it? And when I have built up a sufficient image, I say, "I know her." And she says, "I know my husband, his quirks, his idiocy, his good points," and so on. All that is knowledge. And we are asking, What place has that in relationship? Or has it no place at all?

After all, is love knowledge? Which means the remembrance of sex, of all the background that you have built up in that particular relationship. And that knowledge is divisive, isn't it? It separates. I with my ambition, greed, and all the rest of it, and she with hers. She wants to fulfill and I want to fulfill. So we may meet together in bed, but are still like two rails that never meet. Do we face this? If you are married do you face this? If you live with a partner do you face this fact? Or does one not want to look at facts?

So please find out for yourself what part knowledge plays in relationship, what your experience is, whether it is a hindrance in relationship or a factor that helps you to live together somewhat comfortably, somewhat happily, but keeping a careful distance from each other.

May we go on to other questions?

QUESTIONER: You say there is no path to truth. Is the faculty to see this outside myself? My consciousness and means of perception are entirely within me. How can I go without any means or tools toward an unknown goal? What will give me the need, the energy, to move in such a direction?

KRISHNAMURTI: There are so many things in this question. First of all, as we have already said, the answer is not outside a question. The answer is in the question, in the problem. Let's look at that briefly. We are always trying to find an answer outside the problem that is satisfactory, convenient, happy, pleasurable, and so on. Let us see if we can put aside all this escaping from the problem and look at the problem, look at this question together. Krishnamurti says there is no path to truth. Why do you believe him? Why do you accept it? Why do you repeat it? Who is he to say it? What right has he? Or is he reacting, because he sees so many paths to truth? As long as there are human beings they have different opinions. So it may not be true. Let's first find out.

There are the various Christian paths, Catholic and Protestant and all the innumerable divisions of Protestantism. And there are the several Buddhist paths, also the Tibetan Buddhist paths, though one never really knows what the Buddha said, any more than what Jesus said. There are also the various divisions of Islam. So all these paths to truth, whatever that is, to God, to enlightenment and so on, are displayed before you. There are dozens of them. How will you choose which is the right one? Please tell me.

AUDIENCE: You have to know yourself.

K: Somebody says you have to know yourself. So why bother about paths? Why bother about truth? Why bother about what Krishnamurti says? Why don't you know yourself? And how will you know yourself? How will you look at yourself as you would in a mirror? It is easy to say, "Look at yourself." Socrates and the ancient Greeks, and before them the ancient Israelites, and before them the Egyptians and the Hindus, have all said in various ways, "Know yourself." So there are these paths in front of us. And we all want to realize truth, whatever that is. And all these paths lead to that. That means truth is fixed, right? It must be, otherwise there would be no path to it. It must be stationary, it must be motionless, it must be dead, then there can be paths to it. [*laughter*] No, don't laugh, this is what we do.

Somebody like K comes along and says, Look, don't bother about paths, it may be as though you are on a boat holding a rudder, and you find out, learn, move, keep on going, explore. Not becoming stationary and making truth something permanent. And we want something permanent. Such as permanent relationship. I am attached to my husband or wife, I want the relationship to stay as it is. We don't admit of any change. We *are* changing all the time, both biologically and psychologically, but I want to remain with something that is completely satisfactory, permanent, enduring, giving me security. And when I find there is really no such security, then I have truth as the permanent entity toward which I want to go. And there are all the priests and the gurus offering to help one. I don't know where to, but they help you to it.

The questioner has asked, What are the tools needed to reach truth, which is pathless? The moment you have tools, you have already created a path. Do you see this? The moment I have a means to arrive at truth, the means then becomes the end, and I have already got the truth toward which I am working. The moment you have a tool, a means, a system, you know what truth is, therefore there is no point in having a tool anyway. Do we see this? Or is this too logical? Or too dastardly reasonable? The means is not different from the end; the means is the end.

The questioner also says, My consciousness and means of perception are entirely within me. What do you mean by the word *consciousness*? It is fun if you go into all this. Not only to understand the capacity of one's own brain, but also to delve. We go through a lot of trouble to dig very deeply to find oil, and we won't spend even a second doing this in and for ourselves. So what do we mean by the word *consciousness*? Is that consciousness different from you, from the "me"?

Do you get bored by all this and would rather be playing golf or on a walk or something? Since we are both here, let's go on! What do you mean by *consciousness*? Books have been written about it by experts, and we are not experts, not professionals. We are just inquiring together like two friends. Consciousness is all that you are, isn't it? Your consciousness is made up of its content: anger, jealousy, faith, belief, anxiety, aspiration, all the innumerable experiences that one has had, all the accumulation of the little incidents of life, and also suffering, pain, insecurity, confusion, and the desire to escape from all that and find something enduring. And in it there is also the fear of death and wondering what there is beyond. All that, this vast bundle, is our consciousness. That consciousness is me. There is no me without that. When you say my consciousness is different from me, then you have a battle, struggle, conflict with it, all that ensues.

So our question then is, Is it possible first of all to discover for ourselves, to see that content? It is fairly easy and simple to observe the way you comb your hair, the habits of speech, of thought, and so on. And also to become aware of one's own conditioning as an Englishman, a Frenchman, a Russian, or whatever. It is also fairly easy to see our various religious inclinations, whether Catholic, Protestant, Hindu, Buddhist, or whatever one is following, that too is fairly easy. But to go beyond that, though you don't need an aqualung, you have to go very deeply, and to do that, you must understand the superficial things first, whether it is possible to be free from the influences that condition us. Is that possible?

Find out, work at it, don't listen. Put the tremendous energy you have into it, you don't need more. When you want something you go for it. That means one cannot be rather indolent, one has to be a little active. And there is nobody to help you, no tool, no instrument, no leader, nothing to help you. You must really become *helpless* to find the real thing. When you understand that there is no help whatsoever from anybody, any book, any person, any environment, then something else takes place. Then you begin to see things for yourself.

The questioner finally asks, What will give me the need, the energy, to move in "the direction of truth"? Again, that means it is already over there! I am not being disrespectful or cynical, but when we use words like *direction*, then truth is already *there*. It is already preconceived, already existing, either because of your conviction or because somebody told you, and so on. Truth is really a pathless land. And that can be seen only when fear and all the rest of it is not.

Q: I am afraid to change. If I change, what will happen afterward? I am paralyzed by this. Can you talk about this problem?

K: Why is one afraid of change? What do you mean by the word *change*? One has lived in a house for almost twenty years. One becomes attached to a particular room, to the nice furniture in it. What you are attached to is what you are. If one is attached to that fine old furniture, you are that furniture. So we are afraid to change.

What does the word imply? There is change from *what is* to *what should be*. That is one kind of change. Or there is change according to my old pattern, but remaining within that pattern. Walking from one corner of the field, I say I have moved, and so changed, but it is still within the same barbed wire—enclosed field. Going north, east, west, or south is change. Why do we use that word? Biologically one is told there is constant change in the blood; one cell dies and another takes its place, there is this constant change going on physically. And yet we are afraid to change.

So could we drop that word *change*? Change implies time, doesn't it? I am *this*, I will change to *that*. Or I have been that, and some event will come along, take place, and that event will change me. So change implies a movement in time.

If we dropped the words *change* or *revolution* or *mutation*—all words that the speaker has used—we would then we be faced only with *what is*. Not *what should be*. I am angry. That is *what is*. I am violent. That is *what is*. And to become politically or religiously nonviolent is a change. To *become* nonviolent when I *am* violent takes time, and in that interval I am sowing the seeds of violence. So I *remain with* violence and do not try to change it. I am angry, that is a fact. There are no excuses for anger. I can find a dozen excuses for anger and for hate, but inquiring into why I get angry is another escape from anger. Because I have moved away. So the brain remains with *what is*. Then see what happens.

That is, say I am jealous of you because you look much nicer, smarter, have good taste and a good brain. So I am envious of you. Out of that envy comes hate. Envy is part of hate, and envy is part of comparison. I would like to be like you, but I can't. So I become rather antagonistic, I feel violent about you. Now I remain with *what is*. That is, I see I am envious. There it is, I am envious. That envy is not different from me. Envy *is* me. So I can't do anything about it. I hold it, stay with it. Will you stay with it? Not escape, not look for the cause, or the reason, or try to go beyond it? I *am* envy. And see what takes place. First, there is no conflict, obviously. If I am envious, I am envious. Conflict exists only when I don't want to be envious. I wonder if you follow all this?

If I stay with it, I have got tremendous energy. Energy is like throwing light, focusing light on something, which then becomes very clear. And that which is very clear, you are not afraid of or paralyzed by. It is so. Do you understand? I hope so.

So what is important in this question is not to escape, not to make an effort, just to remain with *what is*. If I am British, I remain with that. See what happens, how narrow it becomes. Apologies if you are British—forgive me, if you are French or Russian, or whatever it is. The thing itself begins to show its whole content.

Q: How does one meet aggression and psychological attack from a close relative whom one cannot escape?

K: Are we all like that? What does it mean to be attacked psychologically, inwardly? When you are with a close friend or relative, there is a psychological, inward pressure going on between the two of you. You know all this, I don't have to tell you. Always trying to do something about the other, attacking subtly, through innuendo, a word or a gesture, always trying to push the other into a certain pattern. This is common knowledge, isn't it? And the questioner asks, What is one to do?

I am living with you in the same house, and you are bombarding me, and I am also bombarding you, not only with words and gestures but even with a look, a feeling of irritation and so on. What will you do not to be psychologically wounded, not to be pushed around? You may depend on that person financially or for various psychological reasons. And the moment you depend, you become a slave. The moment you are attached, you are a goner! Don't look, if I may suggest, at somebody else, but let's look at ourselves. If I am attached to you as the audience, I am lost. I then depend on you for my satisfaction, comfort, reputation, for my physical well-being. But if I don't depend on you, I have to find out why. That means not only I don't depend on you, I don't depend on anything. I want to find out if that is so. I may not reveal this to my close relative.

I want to find out for myself whether it is possible to live in the same house with a husband, wife, relative, and so on, and be totally impregnable. But not building a wall around myself. That is fairly simple: I can build a wall around myself, apologize for it, and be affectionate, but it is still a wall. That means limitation. So is it possible for me to be highly sensitive, and yet not be wounded, not to respond in any way according to attachment? If one is dependent on another financially, that becomes rather dangerous.

If I am financially dependent on you, what happens between us? Most of us are in this position. You have the whip hand, and not only financially. At a deeper level, is it possible to live with another on whom I am financially dependent, and know I am dependent because I can't do anything else? I can't start a new career. If I am quite young I probably could, but if I am fifty or more, I probably can't. So what shall I do?

The question is, Where do I draw the line of dependency? Psychologically I won't depend, I won't depend on anybody, on anything, on any past experience, and all the rest of that rubbish. There is no psychological dependence. But if one is dependent financially and no longer young, where do I draw the line and say, "I have to put up with it"? How deeply do I draw that line? Is it just superficial or at a great depth? What is important in this question, if one understands it rightly, is freedom. Freedom is absolutely necessary. I depend on the milkman, the postman, the supermarket, and so on. Otherwise, psychologically, I don't depend. I must be very clear on this. Otherwise I draw the line very superficially.

Q: Some people seem to pick parts of what you say that fit their problems or interests and discard the rest. What do you say to this?

K: I don't have to say anything about it. What do *you* say? We are all of us dealing, aren't we, with the whole of life, not just part of it, with the immense psychological world and not just physical reactions and nervous responses and memories. That is part of the psychological structure, but there is much more depth to it than that, if you can go that deeply. And we are dealing not only with the psychological world but with the physical violence that exists in the world. The tremendous violence that is going on, killing for the sake of killing, for the fun of killing, not only with the gun, but also the destruction of people when they obey somebody.

Obedience is a dangerous issue, please listen carefully, not taking part of it and saying, Yes, he is against the army. We are dealing with the whole phenomenon of life, not parts of it. Dealing with parts is what scientists, doctors, priests, and educators are doing. We are concerned with the entirety of human life. And if you like to pick parts of it, that is up to you. You find a part that is satisfactory and say, "That suits me, that is enough for me." That is also all right. But if we are concerned with the whole of life, not only one's own but also the life of human beings throughout the world, the immense poverty and all the religious nonsense that is going on in the world. . . . Are you concerned with the whole of humanity? Because you are humanity. It is not that humanity is out there and you are different. We are not British, French, or Russian, we are human beings first, nationals and professionals afterward.

We human beings have separated ourselves from each other, and that is why there is chaos in the world. It is only a war in Lebanon, so who cares! It is just a war in the Far East, Afghanistan, and so on. But if you feel deeply that you are the entire humanity, because you suffer as others do, shed tears, and they do too, you are anxious, laugh, have pain, and so do they, whether they are rich or poor. . . . So we are the whole humanity. If one realizes that marvelous fact, which is the truth, then you will not kill another, then there is no division between one country and another, then your whole life is different, if that is what you want.

But if you want to pick parts of it, go ahead. Nobody is putting pressure on you not to pick a part of it to satisfy your little demands, or your big demands. But if one actually, deeply, honestly, without all the ideological nonsense, sees the real fact that we are representative of the whole of humanity, that believers, nonbelievers, the Muslims, the Hindus, the Buddhists, the Christians, we are one. . . . We all go through tremendous travail. So the search for individual freedom, individual becoming, and so on, becomes rather childish—for me, anyhow.

Q: There are many accounts of people following a particular discipline who come upon the immeasurable. Are they self-deluded? Or has this somehow come about despite their efforts? Or is there another explanation?

K: It is nothing to do with discipline and with effort. You may of course disagree or agree, but let us all understand what we are talking about. You may follow a particular discipline, Buddhist, Hindu, Christian, under an abbot or a guru, follow certain rules, pray at two o'clock in the morning or later. And by that discipline some people say they have understood or realized the immeasurable. The questioner asks whether they are deluding themselves. What do you say? According to the dictionary, the word *discipline* means to learn. The disciple learns, not from a master but by not conforming, not imitating, not obeying. That is learning. Such learning has its own discipline.

That is the quality of learning that is not memorizing and repeating. But most of us accumulate knowledge and memory to do certain functions and use certain skills. That kind of learning involves the accumulation of knowledge and acting according to that accumulation. And knowledge can be added to more and more, or become staler and staler, more and more habitual. So most of us are memorizing in order to have a skill. To live in modern society you must put in some kind of effort, have some kind of skill to work in a factory, in a mine, in business, or at the altar. In the churches, temples, and mosques, you see them repeating the same old stuff day after day. And that is not learning, though they may say it is. But such endless repetition is really rather meaningless.

So can discipline of the kind that means conforming, imitating, obeying, toeing the line lead to the immeasurable? *Immeasurable* means that which cannot be measured. It is beyond all measurement, all delineation. It seems to the speaker that that is not possible, because the brain is then conditioned to a routine, to a certain particular form, and the very essence of the limitless means that to see what it is there must be immense, incalculable freedom.

So what is freedom? There are two kinds of freedom. Freedom from and freedom per se, for itself. There can be freedom from fear, but that is a conditioned freedom because it is freedom *from* something. And is there a freedom that is of itself, the thing itself? That freedom comes about only with compassion and love, and with that supreme intelligence that has nothing to do with the intelligence of thought. And to come to that, one has to be free from all fear. If that interests you, you have to put your energy into it, you have to put your life, your house, in complete order, not keeping tidy, polishing the furniture of the house you live in—though that is part of it—but the inner house, the deep house that has no foundation, no roof, no shelter. And you can't invite the immeasurable—then it becomes a plaything. And you can't lay down the path for another to follow. It is not to be put into words. We measure everything with words. We use a word and call it the immeasurable. It certainly is not the word. It is something entirely different.

# 12 ⑨ LOVE AND THE ENDING OF SELF-INTEREST AND SORROW

WE ARE GOING TO HAVE a conversation in which there is no authority, in which there is no specialist. We are all laymen, and together we are going to talk over freedom, self-interest, pleasure, pain, sorrow, and love. And if there is time, we will also talk about death.

As we said previously, this is a rather serious group; at least the speaker is serious. He has been at it for the last seventy years and more. But just attending a couple of talks or reading some printed words is not going to solve our problems, it is not going to help us. And the speaker is not trying to help you. Please be convinced of that, be assured that he has no authority and so is not a person to whom you can turn to be helped. There are others who might help you. And if you want to be helped, if one may point out most respectfully, you leave your problems to be solved to others, and they will solve them according to their desires, self-interest, their power, their position, and all that business. So we are ordinary laymen talking things over together. We are going to inquire together, face the facts, not ideas about facts but the facts themselves. We are not concerned with ideologies, theories, speculations—they are meaningless. Together we are going to go into this question of freedom, and what relationship freedom has to time, thought, and action. Because we live by action, everything we do is action.

There is a great deal of anarchy, chaos, and disorder in the world. Who has brought this about? That is our first question. Who is responsible for all the mess that we have in the world, economically, socially, politically, and so on, all leading up to war? There are terrible wars going on now. And does each of us realize, not intellectually but actually in our daily life, how disorderly, contradictory, how very little freedom we have, not only in the outer world but also in the world within? That word *freedom* also implies love, not just freedom to do what you like, when you like, where you like.

But living as we are on this earth each of us is seeking his own freedom, his own expression, his own fulfillment, his own path to enlightenment, whatever that may be. Each one has his own particular form of religion, superstition, belief, faith, and all the things that go with it, such as hierarchical authority, whether political or religious. So we have very little freedom. And that word is used so glibly by every psychopath, and by every human being, whether he lives in Russia or the so-called democratic world, because every human being inwardly, consciously or unconsciously, needs freedom, needs to have that quality of dignity, love, just as every tree in the world needs freedom to grow.

So what is the relationship of freedom to self-interest? Please, we are talking things over together: You are not, if I may point out, listening to a speaker, listening to a man on the platform. He is not important at all. And the speaker really means that. But perhaps you can give your ear to what he says as one friend talking very seriously to another. So what is the relationship between freedom and self-interest? Where do you draw the line between the two? And what is self-interest? What is its relationship to thought and to time? Please, all these questions are involved in freedom. Bearing in mind that freedom is not fulfilling one's own ambitions, greed, envy, and so on.

Self-interest may hide under every stone of our life. What is self-interest? Can one consciously, deliberately, inquire into that—how deep, how superficial it is, and where it is necessary, and where it has absolutely no place at all? Self-interest has brought about a great deal of confusion, disorder, and conflict in the world. Whether that self-interest be identified with a country, a community, a family, or with God, with the beliefs, faiths, and so on, it is all self-interest, seeking enlightenment—as though enlightenment is something you can seek! There is self-interest in that seeking, and also there is self-interest when you build a house, have insurance, a mortgage. Self-interest is encouraged commercially and also by all religions; they talk about liberation but put self-interest first.

We have to live in this world, we have to function, to earn money, have children, be married or not married. And living as we do, how deep or how superficial is our self-interest? It is important to inquire into this. We know that self-interest divides people. We and they, you and I, my interest opposed to your interest, my family interests opposed to your family interests, your country opposed to my country, in which I have invested a great deal of emotion and interest for which I am willing to fight and kill, which is war. We invest our interest in ideas, faiths, beliefs, dogmas, rituals, and so on—this whole cycle. At the root of it there is a great deal of self-interest.

Now can one live day by day in this world being clear as to where self-interest is necessary—please, I am using this word carefully—where it is physically necessary, whereas psychologically, inwardly, it is totally abandoned? Is that possible? Is it possible for each one of us living in a very complex, competitive society, now agreeing, now disagreeing, one faith opposing another faith—this great division going on not only individually but collectively—and living in such a world to know where we draw the line between self-interest and no self-interest whatsoever psychologically? Can we do that? You can talk about it endlessly, go to lectures and listen to somebody else, but here we have to observe together, we have to listen not only to each other verbally but also deeply, inwardly, to find out not just where my self-interest lies but extensively, generally, where self-interest lies.

So inwardly, psychologically, can one live without any stirring of self-interest, of the self, the "me," which is the essence of self-interest? Another person can't explain to you or say *this* is self-interest, *this* is not self-interest, that would be terrible. But one can find out for oneself by inquiring very carefully, hesitantly, step by step, and not coming to any conclusion. Because there is nobody who is going to help us. I think we must be completely certain of that: Nobody is going to help us. Some people may pretend otherwise, and you may too, but the actuality is that after forty thousand years, we are still seeking help, and we are stuck. We are coming to the end of our tether.

In the inquiry into self-interest, we have also to go into the question, What is freedom? Freedom implies love; freedom does not mean irresponsibility, doing exactly what one wants, which has brought about such a mess in the world. And also, What is the relationship between self-interest and time and thought?

Time is not only the past but the present and the future, the past modifying the present and therefore modifying the future—the future, tomorrow, is what I am today. So as you are sitting here now, as you are listening, as you are perhaps paying attention, "the now" contains all time. If one really profoundly understands that, then change is totally meaningless. You are what you are now. And to remain with that, not say, "Well, I hope to change. I will become this, I am violent, but I will be nonviolent later." Don't be puzzled, it is very simple. It is really terribly simple, if you come to look at it. I am violent today. We have been violent for the last two and a half million years. We have tried to cover it up with words, explanations, logical conclusions, but we are still violent, competitive, barbarous, killing each other, hurting each other both physically and psychologically. We are violent people. All that is going on in the world: throwing bombs, the terrorism, all the horrible things that are being done to other human beings, the animals.

If there is no transformation now—now, at this moment, at this second—tomorrow you will still be violent. That is logical, reasonable. Do pay a little attention to this, if you don't mind. If I am angry, hating, antagonistic now, I will be the same tomorrow. Obviously. So the now contains the past, the present, and the future. So saying, "I will change" implies a movement in time, right? I am this, but I will be that. That means time, which means I have really not captured the significance of time. But if I remain with *what is* completely, without a single movement away from that, then that which I observe, hold, stay with is me. Violence is not separate from me; I am violence. Anger is not separate from me; I am anger. Greed, envy, I am that. But because we have separated it, there is conflict.

This is all very simple. Is it clear between us somewhat? Not that I am making it clear to you. You are making the thing clear for yourself. It is not a question of you understanding what is being said, or the speaker explaining what he means, so that you can say, "I don't understand you." You are not understanding the speaker, you are understanding yourself; you are looking at yourself, if you are not too depressed, not too lazy, not too concerned with superficial things.

So there is obviously no freedom in this whole cycle of time-thought and self-interest. Where there is self-interest, there can never be freedom. It is so obvious, so simple if you look at it.

And the simpler it is, the more subtle, the more extraordinary depth it has.

We ought also to talk over together the whole acquisitive, pleasurable, gratifying process. It is like digging in the earth to find gold. You don't find it by scratching the surface, you have to dig down very deeply. Not up in the air, in the sky! And, as we said the other day, you are the entire humanity. You don't have to look for another to help you to dig, or help you to go into yourself; you are that, you are the whole of humanity. Because thinking is common to all of us—thinking, not what you think about. Thinking is common to all humans, whether they are scientists, whether they are Tibetan Buddhists, or whoever. They all think, they all have pleasure in sex or in attachment, possession, achieving position, money, glory, fame, and all that business. And all human beings, whatever their race, color, religion, prejudice, all go through pleasure, pain, anxiety, uncertainty, and sorrow.

So it is not your sorrow only, it is not your own particular pleasure, it is the sorrow and pleasure of humanity, right? We have always sought pleasure physically and psychologically, and if we do not find it, we invent something extraterrestrial—like little green men! Sorry to joke about it. So pleasure is sought in acquisition, possession, I possess you, you possess me. Think it over, look at it. And that pleasure is always clouded with fear. So pleasure, fear, self-interest, time-thought are all one movement, not separate movements.

We ought also to inquire into what is suffering and why human beings have suffered from time immemorial. They have done everything on God's earth to escape from suffering, not only physical suffering but also, much more importantly, from psychological suffering. And in spite of all the religions, one particular religion worshiping suffering, as in Christianity, and other religions having other escapes, man, woman has never solved this problem. They bear with it, tolerate it, get crippled by it, shed tears, become psychopathic. And suffering in different forms is common to the whole lot of us. Either you just shed tears, keep it to yourself, and carry on, or it becomes too much. And there is always this killing of each other. Millions upon millions have shed tears from the insanity of war, the brutality of it, building armaments, while millions upon millions starve. I don't have to go into all that, it is all very clear. One nationality fighting another nationality, which means another group of human beings like yourself; you may label yourself British, Indian, or whatever, but you are human beings first.

So we are asking, Is there an end to war, or rather an end to suffering? Because as long as we are separate as a family, as a community, as a clique, as a nation, a religion, and so on, this division will always, perpetually create conflict. You and me. We and they. This is the game we have been playing. First it was limited, tribal, now it is global. So we are asking ourselves, Is there an end to sorrow? Put this question seriously to yourself. Because where there is sorrow, there cannot be love. There can be generosity, sympathy, pity, tolerance, empathy, but these are not love. Love may include or have all that, but the parts don't make the whole. You can combine sympathy, empathy, kindness, generosity, friendship, but that is not love.

So is there an end to sorrow? This requires immense energy to go into, not just say, "Well, I will think about it." Because thinking may be the factor of sorrow. My son is dead, and I have got his silver-framed photograph on the mantelpiece or the piano. I remember him. Remembrance is a process of thought. Of course it is: thinking how we enjoyed the sunset together, how we walked, laughing, in the forest, and he is gone. But the remembrance of him goes on. And that remembrance may be the factor of sorrow. I don't want to admit that my son is dead, gone.

To admit such a fact is to admit utter loneliness. And we don't want to face this fact of being utterly by oneself. And so I look for another. I rely for my happiness, satisfaction—sexual or otherwise—on finding another. And I play the same game over and over again. But I have not ended sorrow—not I, the speaker—but *we* have not ended sorrow. Sorrow is not only self-pity, self-interest, but also the loss of that which I had, also the failure to fulfill, to achieve, to gain something that I have worked for, not only physically but psychologically, inwardly. All this and much more is implied in sorrow. And we are asking ourselves, nobody is putting this question as a challenge to you, but you are asking *yourself* whether sorrow can end. Not only one's own sorrow but also the sorrow of humanity, of which you are. That means no killing of another, no psychological wounding of another. Yes, sirs! As we have said, where there is sorrow, there cannot be love, which is a fact.

So we ought to inquire—not inquire, but look at—what is love. That word has been so misused, so spat upon, dirtied, and made ugly. "I love my country," "I love my God," "I pray for love," "I am not loved, but I want to be loved"—and love poems. Is love sensation? Please ask yourself all these questions. Is love a continuation and remembrance of pleasure? Is love desire? Do you know what desire is? May I go into it briefly? What is desire, by which you are driven and riven, torn apart, what is that thing called desire? Not to suppress it, to transmute it, or do something with it, but what is the movement of desire, how does it come about? Are you putting these questions to yourself, or do you want the speaker to explain? Let's go into it.

We live by sensation, whether physical sensation or psychological sensation. Sensation is part of response, part of comparison and so on; I sense, feel, I sense the atmosphere, good or bad. That sensation comes about through seeing, touching, hearing. And then what happens after sensation? Thought comes in and uses that sensation as an image, right? I see a nice house, a garden, or a nice picture, or furniture, or a nice woman; there is seeing, contact, then sensation comes. Unless there is sensation we are paralyzed—as most of us are! If we don't have sensation in our legs, in our hands, all the rest of it, we are paralyzed. So there is sensation. Then what happens? Thought takes sensation over and makes it into an image, right?

I see you beautifully dressed, clean, healthy, bright, a good brain, and all the rest of it. I see the way you talk, the way you do this and that. Then thought says, I wish I were like him or her. At that moment desire is born. Sensation, then desire, then thought giving shape to that sensation. And if there is an interval between sensation and thought, then you can go into it much more. Are we somewhat together in this? You see, our difficulty is that we are so complex in our thinking, always searching, wanting to find a solution to problems: "How am I to do this?" We are never simple. I don't mean physically, like reducing life to having one macrobiotic meal a day, going crazy about that or yoga or tai chi, you know, the things we play at. We are not playing. This isn't a fantasy, something you are hooked on. This is our life, our everyday lonely, ugly, little life.

So what is love? Can love exist where there is hate and fear, where there is competition and comparison, where there is conformity, agreeing or disagreeing? Go into all this. Or is love nothing to do with all this? Is love something in the brain, inside the skull? Or is it something entirely beyond thought and time? Obviously where there is self-interest there cannot be love. You can see all that for yourself.

So what relationship has love to sorrow? And can love be compassion, not only "I love you, you love me"? Love is not yours or mine, it is love, right? I may be married, have children, sex, and all the rest of it. In all that there may be tenderness, generosity, politeness, kindliness, yielding, tolerating. But all that is not love.

Compassion and love are not separate, they are one. And can one live like that? Can one have this in one's life? Not in occasional moments, when you are sitting by yourself on a sofa or walking in the woods and there is a flash, a scent, a perfume that seems for a second to transform your whole existence. Can we live our daily life with that perfume? For that compassion has its own intelligence. Not the compassion of a man going to India or Africa to do missionary work or help the desperately poor—that is not love. Where there is love there is absolute freedom, not the freedom to do what you like, to assert yourself or convert others. All that silly stuff.

That intelligence is not the intelligence of thought, right? One needs a great deal of intelligence to go to the moon or build a submarine or a computer. But that is partial intelligence. The scientist, the painter, the poet, the ordinary person who bakes bread, that is partial intelligence, not complete intelligence. And that holistic intelligence, the whole quality of that intelligence, love, can come about only with the ending of sorrow, and then that acts, not the partial action that is brought about by thought and time. [*long pause*] Shall we sit still? We can't hold hands. But we can sit quietly for a few minutes. Shall we?

AUDIENCE: Yes.

KRISHNAMURTI: Good. Not *meditate*, just sit quietly.

# 13 ✺ TO UNDERSTAND LIFE IS TO UNDERSTAND DEATH

W
E HAVE BEEN TALKING about various problems that arise in our daily, monotonous, rather pleasure-seeking lives, which are also full of fear, anxiety, antagonism, and so on. We went into the question of time-thought. We have talked about the ending and the nature of sorrow, what it implies, all the pain, loneliness, depression, and uncertainty, and how in some parts of the world they worship sorrow and pain. We have never been able to end sorrow, not only the various kinds of sorrow in one's own life, but also the sorrow of the world as a whole. Look at the terrible wars that are going on, the possible use of the atom bomb. Millions have been slaughtered in the name of God, peace, country, some ideological concept or theory.

This has been our lot, and we have endured all this for thousands of years. Looking at our evolutionary past, we were barbarians, savages once, and when one looks at what is happening now, we are still barbarians, we are still violent, concerned inwardly with ourselves and nobody else, concerned with our own pleasures, problems, and so on. We never seem to realize that we are the world, and the world is us. This is not a theory, not something you think about and come to an ideological conclusion about, or see as a utopian idea, but it is an actuality in daily life. You are the world and the world is you.

One wonders how many of us realize this fact, actually realize it as we realize physical pain, as we feel when we are affectionate, tender, quiet. It is an obvious fact that you and the rest of humankind suffers. You suffer and are violent, and the rest of humankind suffers and is violent. When you intend to do something for yourself and want to fulfill that, you are becoming violent like the rest of the world. We have gone into all this, not only for the past seventy years—I am sorry to point this out—but also now. We actually don't feel, realize in our heart and brain, that we are the rest of mankind. When one actually realizes this, not as a theory, not as an idea, but as an actual, daily fact, then there is a totally different way of living. You don't belong to any country or religious group, and you don't accept spiritual authority, including those who want to interpret what the speaker is saying. And when you really feel that you are actually the rest of humanity, you will never kill another, you will never want to hurt another psychologically, whether consciously, deliberately, or unconsciously.

Please, this is all very serious, it is not just a Sunday gathering, a sermon, or a lecture. We are all in the same boat. We are together understanding the world and ourselves and our relationship to the world—not our responsibility, our *relationship* to the rest of humanity. You all may be well fed, well clothed, with a house or flat and a nice garden, or you may live in a slum, but there are millions of people who are starving, tribes that are being exterminated. And as long as we don't feel all this but merely accept it as an idea, a conclusion, we are going to create a monstrous world, which we are already doing. We are that which is happening.

We ought also to talk about other aspects of our life. We have talked about compassion, love, and that compassion has its own intelligence, love has its own intelligence, not the intelligence of clever thought, calculation, remembrance, but the compassion that can come, or be, only when suffering ends. We talked about that a great deal. The actuality of that feeling of compassion can come only when there is the end of sorrow and when one actually, in one's being, heart, mind, feels that one is the rest of the world and doesn't belong to any sect, any group, any guru, any church, mosque, or temple.

You will listen to or read about all this, which the speaker has talked about for so long, and say, "Yes, marvelous ideas, well reasoned, logical, but . . . ," and you can add many *buts* to that. So we carry on and therein lies more conflict. Or you hear one thing, agree or disagree, or see the truth of it and then want to live up to it, and so conflict starts again.

We went into conflict a great deal previously. And we said that as long as conflict exists there cannot be love between man and woman, between people, nations, communities, and so on. Our brain, which has evolved over eons, has extraordinary capacity. Everyone's brain has extraordinary capacity. We have used it in the world of technology, the world of computers, but we have never looked at the psychological world, which is far more important—the subjective, the whole psychological process that goes on inwardly. We have never looked at that, we have never gone into it deeply, not according to others, including K, but have only scratched the surface. And so we never put fundamental questions to ourselves. And we are now talking over things together—not the speaker saying something and you just listen, and when you leave you forget all about this and pick it up ten years later. This is your life and our life, and one can treat one's life seriously or flippantly or casually, it is up to you.

We talked too a great deal about freedom, freedom from anxiety, sorrow, pain, and all the travail of life. And there is also another kind of freedom. A freedom that is per se, for itself, not because you want to be free *from* something—that is only very partial freedom. There is a freedom that is completely whole, not partial.

And this morning we should also talk about death. We have talked about so many other things. Death is not a morbid subject for a dark morning or a dark night. People have written endlessly about how to die happily, how to accept it naturally, how to let the body go. And now you and the speaker are going to explore it together—please, together, he is not talking to himself, he is not lecturing, not talking about something you need interpreters to understand.

So let us talk over together this very important, serious, very great thing called death. Please bear in mind he is not talking *down* to you. We are talking *to* each other. He has no authority—and I mean that—he has no sense of superiority, no sense of he is the one to tell you all about it. We are going into it together. If you want to. If you don't, that is all right too. Nobody is imposing anything on you, directing you, telling you what to do or what to think.

What is death? When we ask that question, we ought also to consider what is continuity, and also what is ending, something that comes to finality. So ending, continuity, time, thought, and death. All these are involved when we ask, What is death? The urge, the demand for continuity; and when we see this demand for continuity, we should also inquire together what is ending. And is there a beginning? All these are involved in the question of what is death, not just a lack of oxygen to the brain and popping off or kicking the bucket, or whatever you like to call it. This concerns the whole human being: the way one lives as well as the way one dies.

So we are inquiring together what is death. And why death is associated with sorrow. Are you following all this? The speaker is not leading you, he is not persuading you. I am bored with telling you that! So what is death? You must take the whole of it, not just dying. You must take the being born, and living, forty, fifty, sixty, seventy, ninety years, or a little more—you have to take the whole of it, not just limit yourself to asking what death is. It is rather silly to ask what death is and then weep about it, or be frightened by it, or worship it, as Christians do. There are also the theories of the ancient Hindus about reincarnation, which exploded all over Asia, as did those of the Greeks, Pythagoras and others, over the Western world. We will talk about that presently.

So we have to consider not only what is continuity but what is ending, and what part time and thought play in this process. Which means we have first to inquire what is living, not what is dying. Right? Are we together in this? So what is living? What do we call living? From the moment we are born through the long period that we call life, living, what takes place there? Not just part of it but the whole length of it. As we have said, from childhood we have problems. Children sent to school have to learn to read and write, how to learn mathematics and later on chemistry, biology, that all becomes a problem. They are educated in problems.

These are all facts, not the speaker's imagination. So from the beginning our life is a continuous problem, struggle, pain, anxiety, uncertainty, confusion, success, failure, faith, belief, God and the perpetual repetition of rituals, and the worship of a symbol—what is called religion. All that is our living. This is an actual fact, which also includes pleasure, sex, and all the rest of it. This is what we call living. Go to the office or the factory from nine to five, or work in a shop and sell books, clothes, food, and so on. This is our daily monotonous, so-called disciplined life. Would you and I disagree about that? Or do we see it as a fact? Not just accepting this description, but seeing this as the actuality of our life. And it seems we have not understood that. We have not gone into it to see if one can live totally differently.

But there is always death. There is a good Italian proverb,

which says, "I know everybody else will die. And perhaps I will too!" So what is it we have to grasp, understand, go into, resolve first? Life, daily living, or dying? After all, why are we so terribly concerned about death? The speaker was once walking along a shady road in India toward the sea and heard chanting behind him. And there was a dead body being carried by two men, preceded by the eldest son carrying a flaming torch. That was all. Not all the fuss with hearses and flowers, it was a simple thing, and it was really rather beautiful. The son crying, and chanting in Sanskrit, walking toward the sea where the body was going to be cremated. The Western world makes a fuss about death, with Rolls-Royces, an enormous amount of flowers, and so on.

So what are we concerned with? Living or dying? Please, we are talking to each other. Which of the two is most important for us to grapple with, to put our teeth and all our energy into?

Talking of energy, there are those people who want to release energy through acupuncture, and various other attempts to increase it. What is energy? It took a great deal of energy to get all your things together and drive a car here on a rainy, windy day. To decide to come, to sit here and listen, requires a great deal of energy. And we would like more energy. Because we don't know how to use the energy we have. You have plenty of energy when you *want* to do something. They have been to the moon—think of all the technological energy that demanded of everyone. It takes energy to talk, to think, to have sex. Everything, life, is energy, but we, through our self-interest, our specialization, our demand for success, our fears, have restricted that energy. We have made it so small, so particular, so minuscule. Sorry! And our brains have been narrowed down by specialization, by all that business. The energy is there. When we understand ourselves that energy explodes, then you have tremendous passion, not just passion *for* something but the flowering of passion that never withers. And that can come only when there is compassion.

So what are we concerned about most? Death or living? Living is, as we said, a succession of conflict, struggle, pain, sorrow, and all the rest of it. This is not a gloomy picture. You can paint it more beautifully, more colorfully, make it more attractive descriptively, but this is a fact. So shouldn't we understand life, living first, and then come to understand what death is? Not the other way around. What will you give—I don't mean financially—what will you give to find out in what manner you can live totally differently? Not then to pursue some faddish nonsense, like a new fashion of painting, poetry, dance, and all the rest of that immature, childish stuff. The speaker is not being intolerant, he just sees all this going on. So, realizing what our life is, the actual way of existence on this earth, can one bring about a mutation—not just a change but a complete change, a reversal—of the way that one has lived, is living, so it ends completely and something new can take place?

And this means we have to inquire together into what is continuity, what is it that continues in our life, our living. Is it memory? The continuity of the "me," the persona, the ego, is a bundle of memories of a succession of events and experiences. One mightn't like that idea. One wants something more than mere memories, and wanting more, something that is beyond memories, involves another formation of memories, right? One is not satisfied with this memory but wants some other memory. So this continuity, which we call living, is a series, a succession, of events, memories, experience, all that bundle is me, is you. And continuity is that which is known. How scared you are of something ending you to all that!

One has lived a long life of experience, knowledge, traveled all over the place—God knows why, but one has—and you talk, judge, evaluate so much of all that. And we never inquire what continuity is and what ending is. Is it ending voluntarily something that you hold dear? Are we asking each other that question?

Suppose one is greatly attached to a person, or to a conclusion, say historical, dialectical, Marxist-Leninist blah-blah, one is attached to all that like a limpet. Can one voluntarily, easily let go? That is what death means. You don't argue with death. You can't say, "Please give me another couple of days so I can tidy everything up"—it is there at your door.

So can one understand and end that continuity? To us attachment means a great deal. It is the most satisfying common experience—to be attached to the earth, to certain beliefs, dogmas, rituals, habits, and so on. One is greatly attached to a house, to furniture, to a particular habit. Can one become aware of that, and in that awareness end it completely? Not the day after tomorrow, but now as we are sitting here, becoming aware of all that: not the explanations, the description, but the fact, the reality, of this constant demand for continuity of sex, continuity of possessions, continuity of family, continuity of one's deep experiences, all of that coming to an instant end. That is death.

So not to wait for death when you are sixty, eighty, ninety, but live with death now, end life each day. Please, there is something tremendous involved in what the speaker is saying, it is not just a lot of words put together. To live a life that is constantly ending every day, every minute, so there is no continuity of the past or of the future. There is only this ending that is death. *And to live that way.* Go on, don't think about it, see the truth of it. Thought can create, put together a lot of things, but thought cannot deceive death. So if one realizes the immense significance of living with that ending called death in our daily life, then there is real transformation, real mutation even in the brain cells, because the brain cells carry all our memories, the whole of the past. So can we live that way? Not pretend, not say "I must make an effort"— you don't make an effort to die! Unless you jump off the eighteenth floor and then say, "Well, so far, so good!"

Also we should talk together about what is religion, what is the nature of the brain that lives religiously. Religion has become very important in our lives. You may be atheists, you may say, "It is all nonsense, some stupid priest preaching some nonsense." You may shun all that, but yet there is this inward demand, inward asking, "After all, what is all this about, this living and dying, this pain, this anxiety, what is it all about? Who created it? God? Nature? The first cell?" and so on.

So religion is not concerned with all the rubbish, the circus that is going on, whether in Rome, or in England, or in Benares in India, or in the Buddhist countries, all that is put together by thought and therefore very limited. So we have to ask, What is religion and creation? What is creation? Is there a difference between creation and invention? We were talking the other day with an excellent, really first-class doctor, not one who makes money but a good doctor with a good brain. He was saying there is a certain part of the brain that can always be activated. I may be misrepresenting, so be careful, don't accept entirely what the speaker is saying about that. There is a part of the brain that as one gets ill gets a little bit dull, and gets even duller as one gets older. And the question is whether that part of the brain can be revived, made alive. Don't accept it.

So what is invention and what is creation? Religion is concerned with this. The brain is conditioned, shaped, molded by all kinds of things: by your community, what you read, what you hear, the ideas about worship and God or gods that are promulgated by the priests, all that has conditioned our brain. Can our brain ever understand what is creation? Or is it based fundamentally on knowledge, which is experience, gathering, learning, memorizing, and so on? Can that brain understand that which is not measurable? Are we somewhat together in this?

We measure, which means compare, judge, evaluate; we are always comparing ourselves with someone or something else.

Comparing one painter with another painter, one poem with another poem, or Beethoven with Bach and so on—with Mozart, let me include Mozart.

Now, isn't invention based on knowledge? Please, we are talking about this together. If there is no knowledge, there is no invention. We must have a background of knowledge to find something new—but is that creation? Or is creation something totally out of time and thought? This has been probably the greatest problem of a religious brain, a brain with religious quality. In Sanskrit and in good dictionaries the word *meditation,* which is now so difficult to use, also implies measurement. Not only measurement of cloth and material things, but also measuring ourselves against something. Measurement was invented by the Greeks and probably earlier, and without measurement there would be no technological world. And we carry on that same principle in ourselves; we are always measuring how we are today, and hoping tomorrow will be the same or wishing it to be different. There is constant comparing, judging, evaluating. And meditation, that word that has become so mutilated by the gurus with their various forms of it, has become something stupid— sitting in a certain posture, breathing in a certain way, concentrating, and all that, making a tremendous effort to achieve . . . what? . . . A carrot before a donkey?

So we should be concerned not with how to make the brain still—that is fairly easy—but be concerned with total attention, not attention to or about something, but the quality of attention, which is entirely different from concentration. Concentration is effort, focusing on one thing or several things, which becomes a habit like a pilot flying a plane. So is it possible to be attentive? And in that there is no hypocrisy, no pretension. You are attentive. And when you are, in that attention there is complete silence, no border, no "I am attending." There is only attention. Please consider, take counsel together about this.

So what is creation? Not the first cell, nor how we've evolved, and all that. We have said God created all this. On the contrary, we have made God in our image, out of what we are. We have made that poor chap up there! We have given Him all the qualities that we lack: mercy, charity, love, omnipresence, intelligence, and all the others. So what is creation? Can the brain, which is the center of all our nerves, all our activity, all our existence, however small it is, can that brain understand the immensity of creation? Or is there something beyond the brain? Now be careful, please, don't accept anything the speaker is saying. That is the first thing one has to learn, never to accept anything so-called spiritual. That is sheer nonsense. There is no spiritual authority. The authority of a doctor, a scientist, is a different matter. The policeman has authority, especially in Switzerland! Tremendous authority! We were caught in it once!

Is the brain capable of really seeing that which is not measurable? We can talk about it, we can invent it, we can say there is the immeasurable. All that is a lot of words. But we are asking a different question altogether: Can the brain, which is made up of time, memory, thought, experience, all that, can the brain ever understand that which is limitless? Or is there something else, which is the mind, not the brain? Don't invent, then we are lost. We are asking each other, Is there something, which we will call the mind for the moment—we may change the word—is there a mind that is not the brain? Is there such a thing that alone can see that which is immense? And then that mind can communicate to the brain, but the brain cannot communicate to it? Have you understood? We are asking each other.

The brain, as we know, has been reduced to something very small, though it has got immense capacity. The computer is something extraordinary. It will shape our lives, and it is already doing it quietly, slowly; we are unaware of it. We have talked to computer experts who are building a supercomputer. They are not concerned with what happens to the human brain, they are concerned with building computers. When computers take over our lives, what will happen to our brains? The computers will be better, far quicker, so rapid that in a second they will tell you a thousand memories.

So what is going to happen to our brains? Will they gradually wither? Or be thoroughly absorbed in amusement, in entertainment? Please face all this, for God's sake, this is happening! The coverage of sport on television is getting longer and longer. They spend ten minutes on cricket, and two minutes on a serious human conflict. So the entertainment industry is taking over. Please face all this. And religious entertainment has taken over too. So we are being entertained all the time. And you may treat meeting here as part of that. I assure you it is not. It is terribly serious, all this.

So can the brain ever understand the universe? They can say Venus is so much gas, has so many minerals, and so on, but the material description of Venus is not the beauty of it, the extraordinary quietness of it. And to understand all that immensity, can our brain be quiet? Not everlastingly chattering, chattering, chattering. Can that brain become extraordinarily simple and therefore extraordinarily subtle? And if that brain is capable of that subtleness, that immense sense of the great simplicity of time-thought and the rest of it, then perhaps that mind that is not the brain can communicate with it. The present brain cannot communicate with that mind, obviously. Though we do our utmost to communicate with it, all kinds of tricks, all forms of control, sacrifice, taking vows, right? And that thing can never . . . one can never touch it that way. The religious mind, religious brain, always has the background of great silence and solitude.

# APPENDIX

Since Krishnamurti's death, schools that seek to apply his approach to education have continued in India, the United States, and England.

The Brockwood Park School in England is residential, international, and coeducational and provides secondary and higher education for fifteen- to twenty-four-year-olds. The Krishnamurti Study Centre accommodates adult guests who wish to study Krishnamurti's works in quiet surroundings, whether by the day, on weekends, or for a week or so. The Krishnamurti Foundation Trust maintains the Krishnamurti archives and distributes books, and audio and video recordings.

The following is the address for all three organizations:

Brockwood Park
Bramdean
Hampshire, SO24 0LQ
England

Additional contact information for these three organizations is as follows:

Brockwood Park School
Phone: [o] 1962 771 744
Fax: [o] 1962 771 875
E-mail: admin@brockwood.org.uk
www.brockwood.org.uk

The Krishnamurti Study Centre
Phone: [o] 1962 771 748
E-mail: kcentre@brockwood.org.uk
www.brockwood.org.uk

The Krishnamurti Foundation Trust
Phone: [o] 1962 771 525
Fax: [o] 1962 771 159
E-mail: info@brockwood.org.uk
www.kfoundation.org

For information about the Krishnamurti Foundation of America, the Oak Grove School, and the Retreat Center, please contact:

The Krishnamurti Foundation of America
P.O. Box 1560
Ojai, CA 93024-1560
U.S.A.
E-mail: kfa@kfa.org
www.kfa.org

# Notes

## PART ONE

1. STANDING ALONE
From the tape of the talk at Saanen, Switzerland, on 16 July 1972,
©1972 Krishnamurti Foundation Trust, Ltd.

2. LIVING CREATIVELY
From the tape of the talk at Saanen, Switzerland, on 18 July 1972,
©1972 Krishnamurti Foundation Trust, Ltd.

3. IMAGES MADE BY THOUGHT DESTROY HUMAN RELATION-
SHIP
From the tape of the talk at Saanen, Switzerland, on 20 July 1972,
©1972 Krishnamurti Foundation Trust, Ltd.

4. WIPING OUT PSYCHOLOGICAL HURT
From the tape of the talk at Saanen, Switzerland, on 23 July 1972,
©1972 Krishnamurti Foundation Trust, Ltd.

5. The Failure of Education, Science, Politics and Religion to End Human Sorrow and Conflict
From the tape of the talk at Saanen, Switzerland, on 25 July 1972, ©1972 Krishnamurti Foundation Trust, Ltd.

6. Fear Causes Attachment to Belief, Dogma, People, and Property
From the tape of the talk at Saanen, Switzerland, on 27 July 1972, ©1972 Krishnamurti Foundation Trust, Ltd.

7. Living Religiously
From the tape of the talk at Saanen, Switzerland, on 30 July 1972, ©1972 Krishnamurti Foundation Trust, Ltd.

## PART TWO

8. Being Free of Problems
From the tape of the talk at Brockwood Park, England, on 24 August 1985, ©1985 Krishnamurti Foundation Trust, Ltd.

9. The Limitations of Time and Thought
From the tape of the talk at Brockwood Park, England, on 25 August 1985, ©1985 Krishnamurti Foundation Trust, Ltd.

10. Questions and Answers 1
From the tape of the session at Brockwood Park, England, on 27 August 1985, ©1985 Krishnamurti Foundation Trust, Ltd.

11. Questions and Answers 2
From the tape of the session at Brockwood Park, England, on 29 August 1985, ©1985 Krishnamurti Foundation Trust, Ltd.

12. LOVE AND THE ENDING OF SELF-INTEREST AND SORROW
From the tape of the talk at Brockwood Park, England, on 31 August 1985, ©1985 Krishnamurti Foundation Trust, Ltd.

13. TO UNDERSTAND LIFE IS TO UNDERSTAND DEATH
From the tape of the talk at Brockwood Park, England, on 1 September 1985, ©1985 Krishnamurti Foundation Trust, Ltd.